DIRECT MARKETING SUCCESS

DIRECT MARKETING SUCCESS

What Works and Why

FREEMAN F. GOSDEN, JR.
President
Smith-Hemmings-Gosden
A Division of Foote, Cone & Belding

JOHN WILEY & SONS
New York / Chichester / Brisbane / Toronto / Singapore

A Volume in the Wiley Series on Business Strategy

Copyright © 1985 by Freeman F. Gosden, Jr.
Published by John Wiley & Sons, Inc.

This publication is designed to provide accurate and
authoritative information in regard to the subject
matter covered. It is sold with the understanding that
the publisher is not engaged in rendering legal, accounting,
or other professional service. If legal advice or other
expert assistance is required, the services of a competent
professional person should be sought. *From a Declaration
of Principles jointly adopted by a Committee of the
American Bar Association and a Committee of Publishers.*

Library of Congress Cataloging in Publication Data:
Gosden, Freeman F., 1941–
  Direct marketing success.

  (Wiley series on business strategy)
  Includes index.
  1. Direct marketing.   I. Title.   II. Series.

HF5415.126.G67   1985   658.8'4   85-17767
ISBN 0-471-82214-0

Printed in the United States of America

10 9 8 7 6 5 4 3 2 1

This book is dedicated to the 90 million households who truly made this book possible. It was their responsive actions to mail and phone (positive or negative) that provided the benchmarks of what generates more sales. They enabled us to learn "why."

A special note of appreciation goes to Ed Mayer, who first documented many of these reasons "why"; Lewis Rashmir, who developed my interests in testing; our list of clients and Robert L. Hemmings, who gave us the latitude to test; my wife Dorothy, who graciously allows a house full of mail as part of our continuing analysis; and Patricia LaMascus, my assistant, who got it all together.

PREFACE

Direct marketing is a business of numbers. It is a complex and difficult business, but the numbers make it understandable. Since every ad, phone solicitation, and mailing can be measured by the responses generated, certain formulae and principles can be established.

Once you have the numbers, you not only can find out what happened, but more important, *why* it happened.

Understanding these "whys" makes it possible to relate to big businesses as well as small businesses, consumer efforts versus business-to-business efforts, services versus products, and, in short, your type of business.

Product managers, vendors, advertising professionals, and those wishing to start a business can all benefit.

FREEMAN F. GOSDEN, JR.

El Monte, California
September 1985

SERIES PREFACE

Peter Drucker said, "The future will not just happen if one wishes hard enough. It requires decision—now. It imposes risk—now. It requires action—now. It demands allocation of resources, and above all, human resources—now." The Wiley Series on Business Strategy is published to assist managers with the task of creating the future in their organizations.

Creation of the future requires application of the art and science of strategy. Strategy comes from the Greek word "strategia," which means generalship. It has clear military roots defining how a general deployed the available forces and resources to achieve military objectives. But business and military strategy, though similar, are not identical. Business strategy is the allocation of resources to achieve a differential advantage at the time and place of decisive importance. "Resources" may be human, they may be financial, promotional, have to do with unique know-how or have a psychological emphasis. But to be effective, these resources must be concentrated so as to be superior where it counts. This achievement is the essence of any successful business strategy and the theme of the series.

The series will investigate strategy in all of its many facets in business including marketing, management, planning, finance, communications, promotional activities, leadership, corporate culture—to note only those topics under preparation or planned. Its aim is to equip the practicing manager with the techniques and tools he or she will need for the most competitive and exciting period in business of all time.

This book on direct marketing is without doubt on one of the most important subjects in business today. Direct marketing is growing at a phenomenal rate every year. Recent estimates as to annual sales run as high as $200 billion a year. The field is immensely broad, including not only the traditional direct response advertising media such as direct mail, magazines, television, radio, and telephone, but also interactive television, computer ads, and a host of other new media spawned by an ever exploding development of technology. If you are in business today, the question is not whether you will become involved in direct marketing but when. Freeman Gosden's book makes it possible for you to understand and implement this important subset of marketing.

William A. Cohen
Series Editor

CONTENTS

DIRECT MARKETING SUCCESS

ONE

UNDERSTANDING "WHY" IS MORE IMPORTANT THAN "HOW TO"

UNDERSTANDING DIRECT MARKETING

This book should have been written 20 years ago. It would have saved a lot of time and mistakes.

The evolution of books and seminars on direct marketing has followed a classic pattern. First came books on how to write letters . . . business letters, love letters, bill collecting letters, all kinds of letters.

Then came books on direct mail. In addition to letters, subjects covered included envelopes, brochures, how to write a headline, and what coupons and reply cards were all about.

Then, as direct marketing really mushroomed, definitive books on "how to" covered everything from concept to production techniques, to mathematical analysis, to multimedia, to testing. And nobody took time to explain *why*.

"Why" is what this book is all about. After conducting over 100 seminars on the subject and working with marketing, media and creative people, a common denominator came through. It seemed every time we took time to explain why something was done, the understanding was both quicker and more thorough.

There is another reason for knowing "why": *your* project is *different*. Your product or service is never exactly the same as one shown in a case history. If you know why something is done, you can more effectively adapt it to your situation.

One of the great advantages of direct marketing is that it is measurable. It is easier and inexpensive to test various factors, and the results are more reliable because answers are based on what people actually did, rather than what they say they might do. These accurate answers, converted to numbers, form the basis of rules and you need to know them. These rules, in turn, form the basis of "how to" books.

Unfortunately, many "how to" books use case histories and those case histories are hard to relate to. The problem the readers have is that their marketing needs are not the same as General Motors, Chase, Doubleday Book Club, IBM, or anyone else. Also, people entering the field find themselves with a product or service unlike anything that has ever gone before and, surely, always on a much smaller budget.

The giant companies, with huge mailings, can afford more testing than you can because small changes can be leveraged into big dollar savings. But you can't afford such testing and your mailing may be too small to get valid results. Understanding *why* will give you better gut decisions and allow you to proceed without as much testing.

The quickest and surest way to learn what is better for you is by understanding *why*. If readers understand why a principle is stated, they can apply that principle to their own situation. This is more meaningful than a rote acceptance and repetition of what some giant has found out.

Adding to the two reasons we have established for the importance of "why" is a third—*new* ideas for improvement come from understanding "why."

Competition will continue fiercely in direct marketing. Improvements usually come from evolution rather than revolution. New techniques can come from any employee. The chance of developing new ideas is greatly enhanced with a better understanding of "why."

One final note. Promotions, significant raises, and job changes usually come as a result of a very positive feeling about an individual. That individual can better create that positive feeling by having a fuller understanding of what his or her work is all about. That individual should be you. A better understanding of direct marketing will put money in your pocket.

I do not recommend reading this book all at once, but I do recommend that it be read in sequence. While I tried to write each chapter to stand on its own, I find that an understanding of previous chapters does help with a quicker and more thorough understanding of "why."

TWO

BASIC DIRECT MAIL PRINCIPLES

TERMINOLOGY—DIRECT MAIL IS DIFFERENT FROM MAIL ORDER

The first step to understanding direct marketing is to understand the language of direct marketing. Let us look at some of the more important basic definitions.

Direct Mail

Direct mail is an advertising medium. You can advertise your product or service by newspaper (the largest of the media), television, telephone, direct mail, magazines, radio, bus cards, outdoor posters, bus benches, and skywriting (one of the smallest of the media).

Mail Order

Mail order is a method of marketing. You can sell your products or services through a retail store, mail order (delivered by mail, UPS, or freight), door-to-door, home party, or vending machine.

It is important to note that direct mail and mail order are neither mutually compatible nor mutually exclusive. That means you don't have to use the mails when you are in mail order. You can use any medium you wish.

Likewise, your direct mail is not always used for just mail order. It can be used to make announcements, give price changes, for recalls, to build retail traffic, or to build awareness and image.

As an example, let's say you are in the mail order business. You would probably use mail order newspaper or magazine ads, as well as television or radio, to get customers. You would probably mail a catalog to reach present customers.

To build store traffic rather than a mail order sale, you might use a co-op mailing (those bulky envelopes with lots of cents-off coupons inside), a direct mail flier, a freestanding insert in a newspaper, or radio or television.

An average day's mail through the post office would show direct mail being used for many uses: store openings, store traffic, mail order sales, sampling, and so on. . . .

Direct Response

Some feel the best definition of direct response is an advertising technique—any advertisement that contains a coupon, box number, 800 number, address, and/or phone number. In other words, any ad that does *not* mention a specific store or stores.

In direct response you are bypassing the retailer door-to-door salesperson, home party salesperson, or the vending machine. That is why it is called "direct."

Direct Marketing

This is perhaps the most difficult definition to pin down. Industry practitioners have labored and argued for years on the subject without agreement. My definition is simple—direct marketing is an all encompassing catchall that covers direct mail, telephone marketing, and mail order.

A common denominator of direct marketing is that it is data base driven. That means there is somehow a mailing or telephone list involved, either as part of the input (mailing labels, phone calling cards) and/or the output (a customer or inquiry list).

ONE STEP VERSUS TWO STEP

Now that we have defined direct marketing and its major related terms, we must discuss the terms that segment these definitions. We must divide the direct marketing universe into parts that require different treatment from each other. One way to segment is one step versus two step.

One Step

This would be a mailing that comes right out and asks for the order. One responds to the advertising by purchasing something. Examples would be a mail order purchase of a dress, signing up for a book club, or the acceptance of an insurance offer.

The result of a one step is a list of customers.

Two Step

This would be a "lead generation" mailing. The respondent asks for more information, a catalog, or a salesperson to call. No sale is consummated until the person receives the catalog or information and then orders/purchases, or until a salesperson calls in person or by phone and closes the sale. The difference between these two options, one step and two step, is enormous in terms of media selection, offer, and, of course, creative.

Two step is important because advertising is expensive. Direct mail is up to 100 times more expensive than magazine or newspaper advertising. Telemarketing is considerably more expensive than direct mail. In-person selling is even more expensive than telephone selling. The cost of a sales call is several hundred dollars.

Since it often takes several calls or contacts of some sort to close a sale, it becomes much more efficient to have much of this necessary contact come from low cost mass media, television, newspapers, magazines, and so on, and the least amount from high cost media.

Low cost media provides the vehicle for step one. Mail provides the vehicle for step two of the two step concept.

Customers versus Prospects

Any discussion of one and two step programs leads right into the difference in approach between customers and prospects.

You can see from comparative response rates. Let's use a hypothetical response rate of 20% from past customers and 2% from prospects. That means it costs you 10 times as much to prospect and make a sale (response) than it costs to sell a customer.

At a 2% response rate, you have to absorb the advertising cost of the 98% who didn't respond over the cost of the 2% who did. For a customer, absorbing this cost is less painful because fewer didn't respond, and the 80% is spread over 20% responding, not just the 2%. Therefore, you use low cost media for prospecting and more expensive media to close or sell a prospect.

If you are in mail order, you would be using newspaper or magazine ads to obtain requests for a catalog or to purchase a traffic building item you've shown. After ordering an item, the buyer would then be mailed your full-blown, expensive catalog.

In business, a low cost trade magazine ad would offer free information. A respondent would then get an expensive packet of information, and finally, a more expensive salesperson on the phone or in person.

As a rule of thumb, use low cost media to prospect and high cost media to close and generate repeat sales.

THE 40–40–20 RULE

If there is only one rule to remember, it's the 40–40–20 rule, developed years ago by the late Ed Mayer, who was considered to be the dean of direct marketing for many years.

The rule simply states the success or failure of your direct marketing effort is:

40%—The Audience

Specifically, the right audience or the right segment of the right audience. This is true for lists as well as mass media.

40%—Who You Are, Your Product or Service, Your Offer

Naturally, Sears will pull better than Allied Wicket. Your product or service can be enhanced by perception. Your price or deal is *your offer*. Several chapters will be devoted to offer.

20%—Creative, Format, Postal

This includes postage rate, format (that is, letter versus post card), paper stock, color, theme, copy, graphics, and anything else you can think of.

Unfortunately, the 20% is the tip of the iceberg everyone sees. It gets over-analyzed, which is doubly unfortunate. Not only is it less of a factor, but much of this percentage is subjective, which is hard to quantify anyway.

We run a large direct marketing advertising agency. At least once a week some new client calls and asks us to do a great, exciting mailing piece. We must carefully explain that we have to go back to square one and work out the proper media and offer. If those two 40% factors are done properly, the creative is as easy as falling off a log. But, if they are not done properly, the only thing good creative work will do is win advertising awards. Now, let's study this rule in greater detail.

First, there are a few exceptions. One is telephone marketing In telemarketing, the list or audience becomes 60%. Why? Because the cost of each call must include the expensive and time-consuming labor and line charges, making the right audience a more important factor. A good telemarketing closer can do almost anything if the person on the other end has some need or interest. If the prospect isn't screened, all is wasted, including the effort to get through to complete the call.

Who You Are, Your Product or Service, Your Offer

Who you are is important because when buying by mail, the audience cannot see you or your surroundings. The mailing piece itself is the only tangible link. Therefore, establishing a well known name, or association with a well known name, is vital. This is why third party endorsements work. Examples are the insurance offer from some insurance company you have never heard of, but the envelope and cover letter come from a department store you do business with, a credit card you use, or an association you belong to. The endorsement gives this unknown insurance company credibility in the reader's eyes.

The who-you-are problem is often solved by improving the perception. Minsky's Wickets, P.O. Box 479, Broken Arrow, Vermont, may not sound as good as The National Wickets Corporation, 900 Fifth Avenue, New York City, New York. An exception is if you are trying to establish a quaint relationship with your reader. In that case, Grampa's Garage, Middlefork, Iowa, would do fine.

The Offer

This is the most important aspect of this 40% segment. Why? Everybody expects an offer these days. Making an offer doesn't mean you are giving up all your profit. Offers vary. Here are a few to illustrate how different offers can be:

50% off

More information

Save $1.00

Buy one, get one free

One free with 12

Shipping prepaid

Chance to win

Results of a survey

The offers are endless. Again, perception plays an important part. The offer must be perceived as valuable to the reader.

The types of offers that cost the least and can be made to look the most important are paper products: pamphlets, booklets, guides, information, and so on. Once written, information of any kind is inexpensive to produce. That is why you see more paper based offers than anything else.

The Audience

List, newspaper, radio station, television station, or magazine selection is very important. It is much more complex than you think. There are over 35,000 different mailing lists available and thousands of magazines and newspapers.

Rarely do you mail all of a list. There are many selections or combinations of selections that can improve your chances for success. These include geographic selection and taking the most recent names added to a list (because they are known to be at the address and not yet moved, and they have recently done something that puts them on a list you are renting that relates to your promotion). The size of a magazine or newspaper ad is important, as is its color and where it is placed within a publication. Other list factors include selection of the proper names and titles within a business, how much a customer has bought (monetary), how often buying (frequency), and the most recent date of purchase (recency).

Choosing the right selection is as important as choosing the right list. Fortunately, we have ways to find out what works the best. We test.

Creative

For simplicity's sake, let's assume that copy, graphics, format, postage class, and paper stock are all equal. However, they never will be because certain offers have certain needs. A cosmetic mailing needs powerful graphics; an insurance mailing needs motivating words.

Assuming these five elements are equal, using our 20% for creative from the aforementioned 40–40–20 rule, that means that each counts for only 4% of the total package. Clearly not much of a factor.

The mistake many direct mail practitioners make is assuming that nothing can be done about offer, list, or media and that therefore creative is the only area for improvement and should count as 100%. Nothing could be further from the truth.

You've just read a few of the ways that each of these elements can be improved. There are endless others. If as much effort is spent on the media and offer as is spent on the creative-format end, results will be far greater.

HOW DIRECT MAIL AND TELEMARKETING DIFFER FROM GENERAL ADVERTISING

Almost everyone who goes into direct marketing comes from a general advertising background, or a no advertising background. Those without advertising behind them may be better off!

In many ways, direct marketing works backwards to conventional advertising. It's like learning to type by the "hunt and peck" system, unlearning that, and learning the touch system. Let's look at some of these differences.

Direct Marketing Is a Business of Numbers

Because direct marketing generates a response back to the advertiser, the effect of any promotion can be measured. That means testing possibilities are unlimited, and all can be converted to the universal language of numbers.

Direct Marketing is an Immediate Call to Action

This means that you are trying to either sell something direct or get someone to identify themselves as being possibly interested (an inquiry). Either case requires direct action.

In direct marketing, all kinds of efforts are made to get you to respond right now. One of these devices is the *action device*. This is often expressed as:

Limited time offer

Offer expires May 30th

Hurry, while they last

If you act now, we'll give you a free . . .

Our price is guaranteed for 30 days

General advertising is often creating awareness, so when you see the product in a store you will be familiar with it and may try it. Or, when you are in need, you may specifically remember it and seek it out. The process could take years.

Direct Marketing is a Personal Media

If direct marketing can print your name on a label, they can certainly personalize a letter to you. Personalized letters work. Because of a particular list you are on, something is known about you. So, without divulging the list source, they can talk about subjects known to be interesting to that reader. (Note: This is done in general terms. If you have a person's birthday on a list and specifically refer to it, you may get a backlash that could hurt more than it has helped.) If you use my name, you had better spell it right!

Direct Marketing is Targeted

If a product or service is available everywhere and of universal interest, there is no place for direct marketing. The mass media, television, radio, newspapers and magazines are, perhaps, 100 times less expensive than mail or 1000 times less expensive than telephone.

Direct mail and telephone pay for themselves when they can target good prospects. If you are looking for the 1000 bakery owners in Los Angeles, you could use the *Los Angeles Times* and one million people would be exposed to your ad. There are two problems here. First, 999,000 of the circulation is wasted to reach the 1000 bakers. Second, not 100% of the bakers subscribe, read, or are even exposed to your ad. Metropolitan papers are often pleased with 40% coverage. That could mean that even with your one million circulation, 100 of the 1000 bakers you are trying to reach don't subscribe.

Conversely, there are lists of every bakery, compiled from either the Yellow Pages or credit reports. You can even select those bakers who own the largest (or smallest) bakeries. You can target in as precisely as a female college senior who lives in Utah, goes to school in Ohio, and majors in engineering!

Unfortunately, with a selection like this, you may only get one name. You can fall into the trap of over selecting.

Direct Mail Can Tell a Complete Story

An important advantage is to tell a complete story. Some products and services require it, especially new products and services. Complete stories may be told in many ways:

Pages and pages of copy

Many pictures

A swatch of material

A beautiful smelling sachet

A sample

A pop-up three dimensional

If you are introducing a new magazine, it is almost impossible to get the total flavor in this highly competitive field without seeing scores of pictures and features. That is why almost all new magazines are introduced by mail.

HOW MAIL ORDER AND RETAIL DIFFER

When you get yourself, like we do, on all the mailing lists you can find, you tend to receive an abundance of Christmas season catalogs. After looking at over 100 of these, it seems to me that many of those department stores who are mailing out, or inserting catalogs in newspapers, are not reaching anywhere near the potential that the professional mail order catalogers achieve. Let's look at some of the successful elements that the mail order industry learned long ago that retailers should be considering for their catalogs.

1. *You must establish yourself to your prospects.* Even though you may enjoy a well-known retail name, many of the people you're trying to reach with your catalog or newspaper insert are not your present customers. Just because you have a big name with your present customers doesn't mean you have a big name with your prospects. If you did, your prospects would be your customers. There's more to it than that. Each catalog should have a personality area of expertise or theme. You must remind the customer that you are the expert in that area. If it's a gift catalog, stress your ability to select gifts that people want—and at the right prices. When you specialize in gourmet cookware, you must create the feeling that you know more about gourmet cooking than anybody else. You know where to find it, and you know it works. One of the reasons people don't buy by mail is their insecurity about making the decision. If they have confidence in you, they have more confidence in making their own decision to buy something from you.

2. *Repeat your winners.* Most retail catalogs I see tend to go with totally new merchandise every time. But the people who have been in the catalog business for a long time, and who analyze each product's performance every time, have found out that the popular items used once should be used again in your next catalog. Why? Because in addition to all those who did buy the popular item, there are a lot of people who *almost* bought it. They didn't have the money, the time wasn't right, or whatever. But next time around they'll probably make the decision to buy the product. Some of the real experts in the catalog business have learned to successfully repeat up to 85% of their items. Many remail their catalog to their own house list, changing nothing but the cover, and they find the results profitable.

3. *Beware of graphic domination.* Graphics are the key to

good catalog selling, especially during the Christmas gift season, and it's important to portray each item in the best possible light. But don't forget about your copy. It can help sell too. Your graphics are your display and your copy is your salesperson. Remember that one of the things retailers are finding out is that it is more and more difficult to provide good, knowledgeable store personnel. In your copy you can cite key points better than the best floor salesperson.

4. *Take advantage of the bank card revolution to get new customers.* Your catalog is one of the best opportunities you have to get new customers. More and more retailers are taking on the major bank cards, rather than requiring cash, check, or their own charge account. This opens the door wider than ever to successful mail order. By allowing purchase through bank cards, you'll receive business from customers who would have hesitated to deal with you on a cash basis.

5. *Because you're big doesn't mean you don't have to test.* It's quite evident from looking at catalogs that many retailers don't bother to test. The continual testing of products, the space devoted to the product, the list, and thematic approaches are the reason there are so many successful mail order companies. The retail industry should start testing with every catalog they mail.

6. *Make a sale look like a sale.* Some of the recent sale catalogs I've seen tend to be ashamed, in their graphic approach, that they are having a sale. They use very fancy, sophisticated type styles and graphics, and forget about the hard-hitting sales reminders that have worked so well for years. Experts have found that the more your catalog looks like a sale catalog, the better you'll do. Sometimes elements like lower grade paper, black and white only photography, and hard-hitting type styles, will tend to consciously or subconsciously make the reader believe that the items offered for sale really are special values.

7. *Remind your customers.* Your customers and prospects

may forget some of the major reasons they should purchase from you. Don't take it for granted they know that you guarantee everything you sell, that you have an outstanding customer service department, that your policy is that the customer is always right, and that they can telephone you day or night collect or on a toll-free number. Remind them about these things in every catalog, giving assurance that when they're dealing with you, it's going to be a hassle-free relationship. It will get you more orders.

8. *Get more involved with your list.* All of your customers are not the same, and I suspect that over the next few years we will see great strides in customer list segmentation by retailers. Computers will enable retailers to identify and flag customers according to what they've purchased in the past. They will develop catalogs specifically for those markets.

There are some interesting developments going on with major newspapers in the United States, working with department stores to reduce their catalog distribution cost. This is done by taking the mailing list of all households in a certain geographic area and matching that against the newspaper circulation. The department store's catalog goes out in the newspaper at the lower rate, and then additional catalogs are sent on to a mailing list of those prospects who do not subscribe to the newspaper. Using the proper list or the proper list segment can do more to increase response rates than most graphic or copy treatments.

9. *Substitute additional items for nonmerchandise clutter.* Some catalogs tend to go overboard in graphically depicting their merchandise. The background of a Yugoslavian castle becomes more important than what is being sold. These themes are important, but oftentimes depicting well in one or two places will be far more effective than doing it on a piecemeal basis throughout the catalog photographs.

The success that retailers can expect from the catalog field is just beginning to surface. We can see the day when major retailers will do as much or more business with catalogs as they do at the store level.

HOW BUSINESS MAIL DIFFERS FROM RESIDENCE MAIL

There is an entirely different set of rules that applies to business mail as opposed to consumer mail. Time and time again, we see situations where agencies and clients are highly proficient in conventional advertising but who seem to miss the boat when it comes to direct mail—especially business mail. Perhaps a review of these differences may be helpful.

1. *Business mail economics: High affordable costs.*   All good direct mail is analyzed in relation to the amount of dollars affordable. We are accustomed to anywhere from $3 to $30 available for our advertising and promotion per product sold when selling directly to consumers. In business-to-business mail, the affordable number jumps dramatically. We are usually talking about big stakes, a sale that will result in thousands of dollars of ultimate business. It may be the one time sale of a computer, office supplies purchased over the years, a metal building, specialized shipping, or a business insurance policy. Whatever is being sold, the average cost of that sales call is now approaching $300. You can be sure that there are thousands of dollars at stake to risk these high sales costs. It stands to reason then, that rather than spending $2 or $3 per order for mailing, you can safely spend hundreds of dollars *per order* and still have a highly profitable operation. It's not uncommon for a business mailing to go out that costs more than a thousand dollars per thousand pieces mailed, as opposed to the conventional two or three hundred dollars per thousand.

2. *It's not your reader's money.* That's right. When you're communicating to most businessmen or women, they're going to be considering the purchase of your product or service with the company's money, not their own money. Of course, everyone has a budget, but there's a big difference between a company's budget and digging deep into your own pocket. It's much easier for somebody to spend other people's money, so you have a better chance of success when you're dealing with business mail. A good example of this is the newsletter field. There is hardly a successful newsletter that is directed to individuals rather than businesses. There are thousands of successful newsletters that are paid for out of business budgets.

So what you might consider is directing your advertising thrusts toward benefits meaningful to the *superior* of the individual you are trying to persuade. After all, it is that person who will authorize the budget your prospect wishes to spend.

3. *A small universe.* There may be millions of consumers out there for your consumer mailing, but in the business world, you're probably looking at a universe of a few hundred, maybe a few thousand. This makes it much easier to target your advertising approach. There are many more common characteristics and motivations in a small universe than in a large one. You'll get a higher response rate, which increases your affordable dollars.

4. *The name of the game is leads.* If you're selling something that permits you to afford sending a salesperson on a call, the sale is probably worth several thousand dollars. It's hard to expect that an order of that kind could be accomplished by direct mail alone. There almost always has to be a salesperson involved. What you're trying to do is find those leads that will be the most productive for salespeople. You're not trying to sell—you're trying to tease the prospect into getting more information.

5. *The mail order buying characteristic is not neces-*

sary. We've talked before about the mail order characteristic being essential in finding new customers. In the case of business mail, this is not true. This characteristic is unimportant because most business mail is trying to obtain a lead, not a sale. The mail order characteristic is unnecessary to get a lead.

6. *The short letter wins.* In consumer direct mail, the long letter almost always works best. In business mail, often the opposite is true. You just want the recipient to identify himself to you as a prospect. The short letter works because all it is trying to do is get the person to identify himself by asking for more information. Naturally, the information requested is usually attached to the arm of a salesperson.

We've talked about what makes business mail different. Now let's talk about one element that is exactly the same, whether you're trying to reach a business or the general public.

In any kind of mailing, people are people. It's always been surprising to me how often presidents of large companies respond to premiums as readily as the newest employee. That's because presidents are people just as much as anyone else. They have essentially the same motivations, drives, and needs. Obviously, they are more experienced, so you've got to be a great deal sharper when trying to reach their magic button.

By remembering these concepts, you can have your business mail achieve the same successes as your radio, television, magazine, and newspaper advertising.

THREE

WHY DIRECT MAIL IS GROWING

WHY JUNK MAIL IS NOT JUNK

One of the biggest problems for those who are responsible for creating and producing direct mail is to convince their supervisors and clients that junk mail works. It is easy to prove that junk mail works, that people want to receive mail, and that business responds just as well as households. Remember that direct mail is a business of numbers. You know how many pieces you mailed out and how many coupons, orders, or phone calls came back. It is easy to divide responses by pieces mailed and learn the response rate.

You also know how much the mailing cost. By dividing the number of responses into that cost, you know the cost per response. If the cost per response is less than what you have decided you could afford and you can still make your profit, then you have a successful program. Direct mail works.

Look what has happened here. The public, your audience, made the decision if they wanted to respond. If the response is large enough to be profitable for you, then the mail worked. The public, whether businesses or households, has said, "I want what you offered." That is not junk. That is meeting market needs.

Since direct marketing is the only medium with definitive answers for each effort, it is the only form of advertising that is measurable and reports what the marketplace wants. Some have said that responsive direct mail may be one of the few forms of advertising that is *not* junk advertising.

Those who mail are constantly trying to improve response rates by refining mailing lists to eliminate poor prospects, tell their story clearly, and reduce the intrusion. Unlike television or radio, your intrusion is not 30 seconds, 1 minute, or even 2 minutes. Rather, it is 1 or 2 seconds—the time it takes to decide to throw your mailing in the wastebasket.

Telemarketing involves a greater intrusion than mail because the recipients must stop what they are doing and answer the phone. As time goes on, it becomes more self-regulating. Its cost is enormous compared to other media and it must perform exceptionally well to be profitable. That is why telephone works so well for customers, and exceptionally well for situations where it replaces an even more expensive method of marketing—the personal sales call.

The random cold callers seem to, sooner or later, fall by the wayside. At this writing, stock and bond salespeople appear to be flooding the market with an excess of calls to prospects at their place of work. The laws of marketing will soon take effect. The response rates will drop because of too many callers against too few prospects and/or the large profit margins in securities trading that make low response rates allowable will be reduced. Discount brokerage is already accomplishing this.

My point is simply that in our free market system, the consumer is the ultimate decider of effective advertising. Explaining this concept to higher-ups in a company or to clients and customers will do much to break down the junk mail barrier.

Related to this subject are complaint calls, or letters about mail or phone. Some are surely justified. In these cases you had better listen carefully and get your act together. Over the years I have found a strong correlation between complaint calls or letters and unsuccessful mail or phone campaigns. We just don't seem to get complaints about programs the public has deemed successful.

There are those that tend to cloud the issue. Some are hard core direct mail haters whose hobby is complaining about mail. The manner in which most complaints are received often indicates a pattern of religious freaks, antigovernment enthusiasts, and people whose ship may be a little bit rocky.

In business, top management often falls into the one letter trap. If they receive one negative complaint, they feel there are thousands out there who feel the same way but don't take time to write. Thus, very successful programs are often cancelled.

There are ways to answer management who have this fear. First, show them what direct mail programs the competition is doing. Make the point that since this form of advertising is measurable and they have been doing it for several years, it must be profitable for them. Rarely do you have to go past this point to get a go-ahead. If you still need ammunition, talk about the billions of dollars of goods and services sold each year by mail and phone. And the fact that almost every Fortune 500 company, bank, and utility uses some form of direct mail. Another point to use is the history of the Direct Marketing Association's Mail Preference Service. This is the trade association of those in direct mail, catalogs, telemarketing, business mail, and fund-raising.

Under the auspices of DMA, almost every magazine in the nation ran ads offering to take your name off mailing lists or to add your name to mailing lists. There were two surprises—even to the mail professionals. First, less than one in 20,000 responded, and, second, more of those who did respond wanted to be *added* to mailing lists, rather than be taken off. Listening and reacting to the vocal minority can be dangerous.

Let's discuss one other point about junk mail. Some mail looks more junky than others. However, that may be in your mind only.

Using a hypothetical case, we take the same audience and divide it into two equal parts. One half gets an offer that looks very formal, almost like a wedding invitation. The second group receives a mailing with hard-selling graphics, underlined words, and margin notes. The funny thing is, the schlock piece receives a much greater response than the formal piece. Now, which piece would you say was junk?

Taking this hypothetical case to the real world, we find that mailers are constantly testing one piece against another. The chances are, most mail you receive has been tested against other versions, perhaps as many as 50 times. It being a survivor, and just the fact that you received it, testifies to the fact that the desired audience does not consider it junk. In the final analysis, junk mail is mail the reader is not interested in.

The mailer wants to reduce the junk aspect even more than you do because mailers must pay for the junk mail—mail that the reader is not interested in. It is a waste. Waste is reduced by list refinement, better offers, better products or services, and better communication. That is what direct marketing programs are all about.

WHY CONSUMER ACCEPTANCE IS GROWING SO RAPIDLY

Understanding why direct mail and mail order are growing so rapidly will lead to better selection of services, mail order products, and more efficient use of direct mail and telephone.

The rising popularity is a function of a changing demographic and economic characteristic of our society. Understanding the causes and symptoms tells us what people want and why. Here are the major residential or domestic reasons.

1. *Increase in working women.* Well over half the female adult population now works, and the number continues to grow, showing strength in all economic and educational levels. As a result, women have less time for traditional shopping. Convenience and time become critical. Someday someone will come out with a catalog of timesaving products for busy people.

Direct marketing not only offers the convenience of armchair shopping, it permits 24-hour-a-day shopping, seven days a week.

2. *Debit card shopping.* Cash is no longer needed. The populace does not have to plan shopping around paydays. These cards also provide more credit, so more purchases can be made. Most advertisers offer purchases using major credit cards. Banks and other financial institutions find that this extended credit is quickly used up. Fortunately, repayment continues to be prompt.

Offering bank card charges increases the number of orders and the average size, leading to a 10% to 20% increase in business.

3. *Inbound telephone marketing.* The telephone and the debit card make armchair shopping a reality. Telephone orders are a must and will increase total business. The question is whether to offer toll-free telephone calls. The jury is still out.

Slightly over half of the mail order companies offer toll-free 800 number services.

Arguments against it center around how much new business is really generated. If toll-free is just attracting business one would have anyway, it doesn't help. People who are having the better success with toll-free are learning how to sell customers up, sell additional products or services, and not just answer questions.

Parenthetically, we don't think two-way television shopping is going to make serious inroads in the near future because it doesn't offer what consumers want.

Starting with the traditional Sears or Ward catalog, the first breakthrough was having lots of items. Something for everyone. Then came the advent of color photography. Next came more prompt fulfillment, then telephone ordering, and bank cards to charge the orders to. Wired interactive television and telephone don't really add that much. What consumers want are catalogs that come to life. The state of the art in the mid-1980s is data bank retrieval with random access. But random access to a video clip on a product takes far more computer hardware capacity than will be widely available in the home in the near future.

The only way to see film or tape clips now is if everybody tuning or calling in watches at the same time. Frankly, we don't see Ms. America dropping what she is doing and rushing upstairs to see Sears's model black cocktail dresses at 8:05 p.m.

4. *Wider selection.* About the only thing you can't buy by mail is fresh fish! Just about everything else is offered—from nuts and bolts to mink coats. In fact, mail order offers a broader selection than almost any retail store. This broader selection means the shopper no longer has to visit several stores to find what is wanted. Here are some examples of current catalogs:

Over 50 kinds of popcorn

300 parts and accessories just for BMW cars

Over 75 bird cages

2000 different size, style, and color shoes

Over 1000 hardware accessories for antique furniture

No retail store can handle these broad lines.

5. *Central inventory.*   Herein lies the key to why retailers cannot compete with mail order on selection. A broad selection means a large inventory. Somebody must pay interest on the money that represents products sitting on a shelf at a retail store, in a warehouse, or at the point of manufacture. There are hundreds of thousands of these inventories of a given product throughout the country. But, in mail order, there is just one inventory point. That means a very broad selection can be made available. What central inventory and wider selection mean is that products that are hard to find, or lend themselves to broad selection, are good candidates for mail order success.

6. *Shoplifting.*   This is a sad comment. But, at many retail locations, up to 5% of every sales dollar is spent to offset shoplifted goods. The public doesn't have access to mail order warehouses.

7. *Transfer of labor to the consumer.*   The best example of this change in our society, leading to greater use of direct marketing, is the bank teller automated machines. From the consumer's point of view, they are wonderful because you can bank 24 hours a day. From the bank's point of view, they save about 50¢ a transaction because the consumer does the labor of entering the data. Thus, it makes the increased utilization of these machines a very high priority among financial institutions. Direct mail to present customers is an ideal method of communication.

Other examples of labor transfer are telephone bill paying systems and direct ticket travel arrangements.

8. *Telling a long story.*   The age of self-service finds two types of employees in a store; the personnel to bring in and price merchandise and the check-out specialists who collect your money. Unfortunately, there is no one in-between who really understands the product.

The problem is compounded because the demand for shelf attention has dictated beautiful, high impact packages with pictures of beautiful people or things. There is not enough space left on the package to tell the whole story.

Some products demand space to tell a long story, and direct mail provides that platform.

9. *Improved graphic presentation.*   Today's catalogs are absolutely gorgeous. The cost of bleed color printing has dropped considerably, so that outstanding color can be affordable to almost every catalog mailer. The merchandise in a catalog can be displayed far better than in a crowded store. And there is at least a paragraph of exciting description on each item—while at your store there is usually nothing. The pictures and the copy are usually so exciting that you just have to buy it.

10. *Mail order offers better customer service than do retailers.*   Consumers are finally realizing that it's a lot easier to return something by mail than it is to go to the store and fight the hassle of the return. It's just that simple.

11. *People basically don't like to shop.*   It's not so much they don't like to shop, it's that they would rather do other things. Time is becoming more and more important. Since more people are working, there is less time to shop and more need for the family to be together. At the same time there's a boom in leisure activity. That means the family or the individual would rather enjoy their leisure time and leisure time activities than shop.

Changes we see for the *future* relate more to the psychograph area. More will be learned about every consumer from past purchasing habits. Thus, products and services that would appear to be of special interest to that individual will be better targeted.

List refinement improves targeting. Editorial targeting will accompany list targeting, so the message will be as precise as the mailing.

Another area of growth will be follow-up. It was many years before giants like Sears learned about follow-up sales, such as warranty renewals. They then mailed out follow-up reminders to renew. Now they have learned that a personal telephone call to nonresponders to the mail will yield even more renewals.

Magazines have learned the same thing. How many solicitations do you get before a magazine gives up on you for renewal? You probably get five mailings.

Anybody who thinks direct marketing techniques have peaked is not keeping track of the marketplace.

WHY THE RAPID BUSINESS MAIL GROWTH

Understanding the reason for the dramatic rise in business-to-business direct marketing gives clues both as to what products or services work best and how to execute them.

The major reason for growth is the rapidly *escalating cost of a personal sales call* (now well over $200 and approaching $300 per sales call). A way had to be found to reduce these calls. Combine this with the fact that over 80% of sales require more than four sales calls. That is what a massive test by a leading sales trade magazine reported.

If the average in-person sales call costs $300, the average phone sales call $8, and the average business-to-business direct mail piece 50¢, then it makes sense to substitute the lower cost medium for the higher cost medium whenever possible.

There are many ways mail and telephone can help reduce the number of in-person sales calls. One is to identify prospects. Another is to "soften up"—or provide precall information, so that the awareness, knowledge, and understanding of the subject is comprehended beforehand. This reduces expensive telephone time and helps screen out poor prospects. There are other reasons business mail is popular.

1. *Nobody likes to make cold calls.*   Once when I made this statement in front of a large sales audience of a multibillion dollar corporation, I got glassy stares from the audience. Suddenly an older gentleman stood up in my defense and said that in all his years he had never found anyone who really liked to make cold calls (that is, calls where the caller is a total stranger to the person called, as is the subject). The audience's expression changed from doubt to acceptance. This gentleman happened to be the head of sales of a *billion* dollar operation. A lead or inquiry for mail or phone turns a cold call into a meaningful prospect wanting to know more.

2. *An opportunity to tell a complete story.*   Personal sales calls are necessary because most business sales are higher priced products or services. Much more time goes into the decision. The better practitioners in direct marketing have learned how to tell these complete stories by mail and get an order directly.

3. *The need to reach more people in the same company.*   The larger the company, the more business it does. Unfortunately, the larger the company, the more people involved in decision making. No longer can one person make a decision or a purchase. Mail reaches multiple influencers, as discussed elsewhere.

4. *People don't have time to see salespeople.*   There is no way around it. A personal visit takes up more of the customer's time than a phone call, and the phone call takes up more time than a direct mail message. That is why routine sales calls (that is, replenishment of office supplies) are now more efficiently done

via a phone call or a direct mail office products catalog. Time savings on both sides—seller and buyer—make direct marketing an effective tool for both.

5. *The need to reach very small audiences.* Not everyone is interested in a $150,000 spectrometer for quality control of iron alloys. Mass media offer 99% + waste circulation where readers have absolutely no interest. Trade magazines are often sub-scribed to but not always read. Targeted mail by industry classi-fication, company size, and geographic area makes sense.

6. *The need to communicate a complex story.* Short letters are better, but sometimes a very complex story must be told just to get a lead or a request for more information. Other media cannot offer the long story capability.

There are many more reasons with lesser effect, such as per-sonalization, lack of sales capability in an area, need to target response dates to a travel schedule for different areas in order to schedule appointments, and the need for quick dissemination of information.

You can probably come up with many more. Knowing the use others find for direct marketing will suggest uses to you. Read your business mail to find them.

FOUR

THE WHY OF
MARKETING

WHY OFFERS ARE SO IMPORTANT

The biggest single error we find in business-to-business mail, as well as consumer mail, is the lack of an offer. Yet, as we have seen from our 40–40–20 rule, the offer is responsible for more of our success or failure (40% of either) than the whole creative area, which only accounts for 20%.

The main reason offers are so important is that the public has been thoroughly conditioned to offers by every other marketing avenue and through all advertising mediums. The public *expects* an offer. They have probably already heard about your product from mass media exposure, word of mouth, shelf exposure, or whatever. Up to now, they have failed to respond to whatever exposure they have had. With nothing different, why should they act now?

Direct mail and direct marketing efforts, via other media, have the assignment to *sell*. If you want to make a sale, you'd better make your reader or viewer take action *now*. The method that works best has proven to be an offer. Offers are many things: sale price, limited time offer, discount, 2 for 1, 1 free with 12, a free booklet, more information, prepaid shipping, coupon good against purchase, limited availability and so on. The types of offers are almost limitless.

Upon learning of the offer the reader is more apt to follow human instincts and take advantage of a good deal. However, this requires that the urge to action more than offsets an equally important human instinct to do nothing—procrastinate and not buy. One of the main reasons people procrastinate is because they are unsure of themselves. They are afraid of making decisions. Even worse, they are afraid of making the *wrong* decision.

By taking advantage of an offer, they may be saying to themselves: "I may be making a poor decision, but the fabulous offer more than justifies the risk." In short, it could psychologically cover a list of sins.

The problem with offers is that they are expensive! This is not true. The real problem with offers is that they are *perceived* to be expensive. Too many marketers feel they can't afford an offer. The truth is offers can cost you almost nothing.

Obvious offers that cost essentially nothing are the empty seat on a plane, vacant cabin on a cruise, giving away merchandise that you can't sell, distributing literature that you've already printed too much of, discounting merchandise that is priced too high anyway, and leftover samples. I'm sure you can think of several in your own business. The trouble is, you've never perceived these useless items as potential candidates for an offer.

Notice the word "perceived." That is the key to anyone who has ever been responsible for developing offers. An offer does *not* have to be perceived as valuable. An offer *does* have to be perceived as needed.

There are lots of things I need that really have no value—information heads that list. Information comes on top because it has a low cost—a few printed pages. That is why booklets are so popular. The problem is that most booklets have the wrong title, as they are usually already printed.

Let's take a hypothetical case of the World Widget Company selling a piece of equipment to businesses. Which of these titles is most appealing?

1. The World Widget Company (You'd be surprised how many booklets just have a name!)
2. A Catalog Of Widgets
3. The World's Largest Widget Selection
4. 10 Ways Widgets Can Improve Your Business
5. How To Get More Widgets For Less Money

As you have probably surmised, titles #1 and #2 are rather lifeless. There is not much motivation to pick up a pen and send for something. The last three titles seem to have more impact, yet each is different. The catalog appeals to those who are already using widgets or have made a commitment to use them. It offers selection. The fourth headline might appeal to those who are just starting to think about widgets. And the last headline is for those already purchasing widgets—like everybody, they are looking for a deal.

The skillful development of the offer means you mail different headlines to different markets, or encompass two or more to a universal audience to make sure you reach as many situations as possible.

Offers work because they are carefully thought out and give the strongest impact to the broadest possible audience. They deserve at least twice as much attention as copy and graphics. If marketers gave half as much attention to offers as they give to copy and graphics, most would enjoy far greater response.

WHY PUT THE PENCIL TO THE NUMBERS—FIRST

Direct mail is expensive. Telemarketing is even more expensive. You cannot afford to waste your advertising dollars at any time, but certainly not when the chips to play the game are so expensive.

Few people go all out and mail large quantities, or make a large number of phone calls, before they have properly tested and learned that what they are doing is at least a break-even proposition. Maybe that is why we can determine "par" in direct marketing in a *break-even analysis*.

You know your advertising cost and what you can afford to obtain an order or a lead. By dividing what you can afford to spend at break-even for an order into your advertising cost, you know how many orders you have to get to break even.

For example, let's assume your advertising cost is $10,000 to mail 20,000 pieces, and you can afford to spend $10.00 to get an order. Your break-even is a 5% response rate:

$$\frac{\$10,000}{\$10.00} = 1,000 \text{ orders per 20,000 pieces of mail}$$

$$\frac{1,000}{20,000} = \text{is a 5\% response}$$

Unless you are pulling better than a 5% response—or if you can see your way clear to do that in the future—you have a losing business proposition.

Knowing what "par" you must reach with any direct mail, catalog, or telephone operation is vital in knowing what to do next. If you aren't getting a 5% response in our hypothetical case, you could do any one or combination of these things to get to or surpass break-even and make a profit.

1. Raise your price so you can afford more promotional dollars per order.
2. Lower your costs so you can afford more per order.
3. Try different lists or segments of lists to get a higher response rate.
4. Improve your offer to generate a better response rate.
5. Improve the impact of your creative effort.
6. Improve the size of your average order so you have more to spend.

This last item, average order size, is a new wrinkle we've added which deserves special comment.

WHY AVERAGE ORDER SIZE IS IMPORTANT

It stands to reason that, if your advertising cost and response rate are fixed, and your gross margin is the same, a $60.00 order will generate more contribution to profit than a $10.00 sale. It will be more than six times as much.

Sales	$60.00	$10.00
25% cost of goods	($15.00)	($ 2.50)
Cost of advertising (50% sales)	($25.00)	($25.00)
Contribution	$20.00	($17.50)

A contribution of $20.00 is acceptable. A loss of $17.50 obviously is not. That is why you often hear the expression, "You can't make any money on a sale under $19.95." As inflation continues, that is, perhaps, a low figure. Many catalog professionals use a figure of $50.00 on an average order size to make any money, which is why low priced gifts and gadget items have dropped out of the mail order scene.

There are several ways you can get an average order size up:

1. Increase price
2. Increase the quantity of units sold per order
3. Make a sale that reaps continuing income (that is, magazine subscriptions, book clubs, or insurance policies)
4. Increase the average selling price of your line of merchandise (that is, go to the upper end of the market)
5. Offer a promotion to encourage larger orders, such as: a free widget with every order of $100 or more. (Don't forget to factor in the cost of the free widget.)

YOU DON'T HAVE TO SHOW A PROFIT IF . . .

Believe it or not, most people do not show a profit at the start of their business. And most professional mail order experts don't show a profit on new customer acquisitions.

You lose money attracting donors or customers because you know you are going to more than make up for the cost by the profit you will generate from future orders from that same customer.

Not only is that customer probably going to buy more from you as he or she gains confidence in your product and its prompt delivery, but your cost of advertising to present customers is only 1/10 or 1/20 the cost of getting a new prospect.

As you progress, you will put your pencil to more and more numbers: response rates, average orders, number of orders per year, average size of order, and number of years they will continue to order. Fund-raisers note that the same applies to donations.

In lead generation business mail, the numbers are often not as critical as in consumer mail because the selling price of the item is usually much greater and the size of the mailing smaller.

WHY BUDGETING IS SO VITAL

There are many unique advantages direct mail has over other media but budgeting is not one of them. However, with a moderate amount of technique blended with anticipation, it can be done with minimum effort.

In all the forms of advertising, the production of advertising is a minor factor. The big hunk is space costs, radio time, or television time. Rate cards and deals are usually known ahead. Even if not, you can usually switch a little bit of "this" with a little bit of "that" and come out okay.

Direct mail, on the other hand, is all production cost except for postage, which is usually one third to one tenth of total cost.

Further, no two printing quotes are the same. There are a million variables, such as number of pieces included, size of each piece, paper quality, and color. All of these vary drastically, based on quantity.

So, you have relatively fixed rates in conventional advertising and the opposite when you use direct mail.

Direct Mail Budgeting Made Easy

Below are nine steps. If you follow each, you are probably in much better shape from a budget point of view than your other forms of advertising.

1. *Know the quantity you will mail.* This is the biggest variable factor by far. It is of enormous importance to creative people. They must know over what size base the creative work must be spread. Usually the larger the mailing, the more you can spend for creative development and finished art because the cost is spread over a larger base.

This leads to the question as to how to find out how many pieces you will mail. When mailing to the general public, follow the principle of the direct mail/mail order industry: You want to mail as much as is profitable. For business mail it is usually different. There is usually a small fixed market of firms out there that could be prospects. If you mail to carpet manufacturers, for example, there are only 223 in total!

Follow this rule: If you have very few prospects, mail them all. If you have lots of prospects (lucky you!) figure a quantity that will give meaningful results to your test. In direct mail, *every* mailing is a test. As a rule of thumb, you need at least 100 responses on the weakest side or panel of a test. What does that mean? Simply pick the one element you think will do the worst. Make sure you'll mail enough to get 100 responses.

2. *Budget your mail package cost in terms of known popular formats.* You must have some idea as to the type of mailing you

want. For example, an outer envelope, two-page letter, response card, and a two-color, six-panel brochure is a fairly standard item. Obtain an estimate but don't limit your creative people. Give them latitude to come up with what will work best with the theme and data to be included. It is much easier to plan by adjusting off a known base. Plus, you can give and take. For example, add a color and compensate by a reduction in size.

3. *Stay away from "pioneering."* Rather than developing some new mailing concept in terms of format, stick to basics. First, determine that the other elements (product or service, offer or deal, and mailing lists) are correct or within range. Test these elements with a basic package; then, once you know where you are, test themes and formats.

4. *Set a test budget as a planned expense.* In direct mail, you will always be testing. That means you will experiment with small quantities to make sure that you are right with large quantities. It costs more to do anything in small quantity. So, budget the premium for small quantities as a planned expense. Set aside amounts you can use all year round for testing. It is the testing funds that will really be responsible for your future successes.

5. *Anticipate inflation.* It makes common sense, but we see many mailers taking today's costs and assuming they will be good for a whole year. Be realistic.

6. *Include peripheral costs.* Careful budgeting for mailing is for naught if all the costs are not included. Don't forget such items as cost of the free premium booklet you are offering by return mail; business reply card postage; cost of fulfillment; cost of test analyses.

7. *Budget your time.* Since direct mail is measurable and is a business of numbers, why not figure in all the costs? That means including the share of your time, your associates' time—from meetings to purchasing quotes to printing, and mailing supervision.

These costs will be incremental, since you are already there. As an alternative, figure a flat percentage of sales to cover this type of overhead.

8. *Include a contingency.* Ten percent is a good average number to allow for Murphy's Law: What can go wrong will, at the worst possible time. More things can go wrong with direct mail than other forms of print advertising because there are more parts. Magazines and newspapers do the production and distribution for you. In direct mail you are on your own.

9. *Make sure you can use responses.* This should probably be number one. Can you properly fulfill the orders generated? If not, don't mail. Save your whole budget unless you can do it correctly.

Follow these guidelines and you will make direct mail even more effective with the type of products best suited to the medium and the right audience. And, more than you can expect from any other form of advertising, you'll know exactly where you are.

WHY PERCEPTION IS MORE IMPORTANT IN DIRECT MARKETING

Selling retail, the customer can see, feel, and touch. See, feel, and touch applies to purchases, repurchases, and returns.

In direct marketing, eliminating the *wrong* perceptions is the first step—creating positive new perceptions is the second step. What are some of these wrong perceptions?

1. *It won't fit.* Frankly, the customer may be right, for there is no better or worse chance it will fit than when you read

a size tag on a rack in a store. Mail order professionals have eliminated this problem by one-size-fits-all (wrap arounds, muumuus, stretch socks, etc.), broad size ranges (S, M, L, XL), child sizes based on age, height, or weight, and ring sizes based on an enclosed diecut set of holes you slip your finger into.

Most size problems are eliminated because the mail order firm develops a *perception* that if it is not exactly right you can send it back.

2. *The color probably won't be right.* Science says color perception is very subjective. There are several ways to solve this problem:

A. Use basic colors only.

B. Include multiple colors in your product (that is, several cosmetic lip, eyeliner items).

C. Use high key color photography.

Again, perception plays an important part. The direct marketing selling copy and the copy accompanying fulfillment tells the recipient that this is the right color for them and for today's fashions.

3. *It won't work.* Electronics, gadgets, certain housewares, and toys all fall into this category. Perception's role here is to assure the prospect it will work by using brand names, executing meticulous quality control, and staying away from products with a high trouble ratio. Still, perception must be developed that convinces the reader or listener that the item really can be returned with no questions asked.

The guarantee is perception's best friend. Guaranteeing your product or service guarantees the perception that eliminates fear of wrong size, color, or the possibility that the product won't work. That is why *unconditional* guarantees tend to increase response rates even further. The unconditional guarantee takes the remaining doubt out of the prospect's mind. That is why the successful firms always include an unconditional guarantee, and make certain it receives important positioning in the communication.

4. *It will take too long to receive.*   The best way to eliminate this fear is to ship your product or service quickly. That doesn't solve the problem for the person who has never done business with you before.

   You must include positive perception copy in your advertising. Many little things add up, like (1) "guaranteed delivery for the holidays," (2) stamping "RUSH" on your order form, (3) preclearances, such as a credit clearance, and (4) "limited time offer."

5. *It is too complicated.*   Banks, thrift organizations, insurance companies, and loan operations have done much to create this problem—and are now doing much to correct it. It all centers around response documents: order forms, response cards, coupons, reply envelopes, and applications. Your customers are people, and people shy away from things they feel they cannot do. Many perceive they can't fill out a complicated order form. All kinds of excuses are voiced, with "I don't have time" probably being expressed the most. It is a great excuse.

   Lawyers and regulatory agencies have dictated that forms to fill out must be complicated. There are several ways to develop a positive perception that will do much to eliminate this hesitancy.

   Tell them it is as easy as 1–2–3 to fill out the form. If you tell them it is easy, they will believe you. Spending a lot of time on your firm's graphic presentation is usually more than worth the time involved. Carefully constructed graphics make complicated forms look easy.

An important part of your simplicity program will be to find out how much data is really needed. This means arguing it out with lawyers and those product managers who say, "this is the way they want it." The use of a readable type face helps.

HIDDEN PERSUADERS

Up to now, we've talked about perception devices that we don't want hidden—devices we want *emphasized.*

There are little things you can do to develop a positive perception. Also consider that you can go too far and promise (through perception) much more than you will deliver. The backlash could do you more harm than good.

1. *Show the product at its most beneficial stage.* If it is a gourmet custard maker, show the finished, gorgeous custard. Your customer is buying beautiful, great tasting custards, not custard makers.

    If you are lending money, show what money will buy.

    If you are selling insurance, give a feeling of protection. Certificates, pictures of happy families, and guarantees all do that.

    Naturally, clothes look nicer on pretty people; table settings look better in an entertainment mode; and toys look better when children are playing with them.

    It all comes down to this principle. Whatever you are offering will be perceived differently by every reader, based on their experiences or needs. Showing off the product or service in a positive way—the way you've found it to be best received—is the perception you want to give.

2. *If you can't do it well, do it differently or not at all.*
Sometimes what you have to sell just can't be photo-
graphed. If that is the case, go to illustrations. You can
often exaggerate an illustration to make your point. Since
it is a drawing, the public will give you wide latitude, realizing that you are making a point.

For those doing real estate, facility brochures, or annual
reports, if you want buildings to look bigger, always crop
the picture *before* you come to the corner or wall. That
corner or wall puts an end to perception. If they are not
in the picture, the viewer perceives that there is an exten-
sion.

3. *Be perceived to be an expert.*   People develop better feelings about products or services if they believe they are
communicating with experts. Since most people don't
know who is an expert in what, good direct marketers make
the perception that they are experts—which, in fact, they
probably are—by just being in the business. Phrases like
"noted authority on . . . " work well.

4. *Above all, be perceived that you care.*   It takes such little
effort and it goes so far!

WHY STORES AND CATALOGS
GO TOGETHER

All things being equal, if you own a store you have a better chance
for success in mail order. All things being equal, if you have a
good direct mail business, you have a better chance for success
in retail. In fact, things don't have to be very equal!

Why is this mail order/retail relationship so important?

1. *Common inventory.* Before you even start expanding into the other marketing channel, you have the opportunity of having one inventory base. This alone can save you thousands of dollars.

2. *Advance knowledge of what sells.* Through either channel you've been exposed to what customers want. This knowledge is invaluable because the customers aren't changing—just the way in which you reach them is changing.

3. *Advance knowledge of vendors.* Who sells what, volume discounts from the other channels, and special relationships for faster delivery are all a help. Just finding out where to buy something you wish to sell is often far more difficult than one would think. These advantages become even more important when imported merchandise is considered.

4. *Proven advertising techniques.* When you've sold through one channel, you have to learn what advertising communication is most effective, which products or services are best helped with advertising, and which media are most effective. Marketers spend years trying to figure out what *you* already know.

5. *Advertising of one channel helps the others.* No matter which channel you started with, you will have some sort of name and reputation. These will precede you because you will be going to the same segment of the audience. Taking advantage of this reputation can mean the difference between success or failure for either or both of the ventures.

6. *Catalog remnants can be sold in stores.*   Without a store, there is nothing worse than having just a few of something left. Too many to discard. Too few to offer in the wide distribution of your catalog. Just the right amount for retail.

7. A *way to get business from out-of-town customers.*   At retail you have both out-of-town customers and people who have moved away. You've built a reputation with them. Mail order provides a method to continue to obtain profitable business from them.

8. *Your catalog is charged on an incremental basis.*   If you are already in mail order, your catalog will be your main form of advertising. If you then open a store, you concentrate more catalogs into that area. You should only have to charge the incremental print run cost, postage, and lists against those catalogs. This should give you an advertising efficiency advantage over non-mail order retailers.

9. *Offering your customers an alternate shopping method will get you business that would have gone elsewhere.*   Your regular retailer may be confined, too busy to shop, or living for six months somewhere else. Your mail order customer may prefer to see-feel-touch on certain items, or may need a further explanation of the product.

10. *Retail site selection.*   Your pattern or density of mail order customers tells you where to put stores. This rather easy research is best done by comparison. Take your list and the subscription list of the publication that best represents your market. Compare these two on a zip code by zip code basis.

      You need to know the universe or population you mailed to, to determine the percentage of penetration you would expect. Where you have the best penetration, and the market is large enough, will be the places you have the best chance.

Most of the people who are doing well in retail or mail order have expanded into the other channel. Most result in success stories.

Why do you need to think of both channels when starting? It might be best for you to do both at the same time. There are so many common aspects, as we have discussed previously, that it doesn't take double the effort. This also gives you the chance to consider buying a mail order company and expanding it into retail, or taking on a retail operation and expanding it into mail order. You are also reminded that if your idea for mail order can't be translated to retail, you reduce your chance for success. This does not necessarily hold true if you are in retail or are considering expanding into mail order.

FIVE

PRODUCTS
AND SERVICES

WHY SOME PRODUCTS
AND CATALOGS DO BETTER
THAN OTHERS

Nobody can be perfect in selecting merchandise or, on a larger scale, deciding on a whole catalog concept or new mail order business.

The great catalogers, like baseball players, are playing the averages. And great baseball players hit less than .400. In addition, 20% of the merchandise often accounts for over 80% of the business.

So what the wise merchandiser wants to do is beat the averages.

To look at some ways to beat these averages, let us divide this subject into two areas: (1) why some lines of merchandise do better (that is, whole catalog concepts), and (2) why certain products within a catalog do better.

These thoughts will be based upon analysis of both catalog merchandise and previously tested direct marketing offers. Some of what can be learned from premiums can be used to select catalog merchandise.

Why Some Catalogs or Lines of Merchandise Do Better

We are *not* talking about the variation within one line of merchandise, between its books (catalogs) mailed throughout the year. We are talking about why some companies or lines do better.

1. *Match lists to merchandise.* The ideal situation is to find a large group of lists of people who have the mail order characteristic (that is, buy by mail) and who have a specialized interest. Examples would include magazine subscribers to specific types of apparel and certain hobbies. It could be argued that you should first select your easily identifiable market and then sell them what *they* need.

Examples of concepts that might fail would be products for left handed people or desserts by mail. These are good ideas, but few lists exist in these areas.

2. *Offer a broad selection not available at retail.* My favorite example is bird cages. There is a catalog containing over 100 bird cages. At retail, pet stores may have only 10 or 20. If you go to different pet stores, you get a lot of duplication, so you could never see 100 different cages. Here is a case where you can't beat shopping at home from a catalog with a larger selection.

Another example is the brass furniture hardware offered by mail. No hardware store could afford to inventory all of these rarely used items. With one central inventory and a list of customers who are interested in these items, you can be successful.

There are book catalogs with thousands of titles.

3. *Odd sizes.* This represents big business for many successful catalogs. Retail outlets can't afford to keep large inventories of merchandise where there is not much demand. Clothes for the too tall, too short, and too fat are popular categories. I suppose there is no such thing as being too thin!

This odd size concept holds true for shoes too. There are over a hundred sizes of shoes. When you add color and style, the combinations are almost endless. The one central inventory of mail order can handle these, especially when they target to these extreme audiences. They don't have to carry the large middle group that you can easily find in any retail shoe store.

4. *Your line must be easy to explain.* If you are introducing new concepts, mail order may not be the way to go. In addition to offering selection, you have the additional burden of explaining what the concept is, proving they need the item, and proving it is affordable. You have the additional problem of being a pioneer. And you already know the saying: "You can always tell a pioneer by the arrows in their back."

The above is not in conflict with a statement we have made elsewhere—that you use direct mail and mail order newspaper and magazine ads to communicate the complex stories that are essential with some products and services.

These complex stories are usually explained in large size ads or in a solo mailing (that is, one product or service). We are talking here about catalogs, where the prime feature is breadth of selection.

5. *Your catalog items should be related.* There are probably more failures due to efforts to sell new products in unrelated areas to present customers.

Because your customers like your Early American furniture does not mean they like your gourmet cooking products. Because you sell auto parts does not mean you can sell travel services. If you sell housewares, this does not mean you can sell cosmetics to the same market.

Why? The answer probably lies in the customer's perception of you. They have confidence in what they are already buying from you. You have yet to prove yourself in other areas. You wouldn't go to your family doctor with a toothache.

You can hedge your bets by gradually moving into these areas. Insert one or two products at a time. You'll see how well you are accepted and you'll start building up a group of satisfied customers in these new areas.

Why Some Products in a Catalog Do Better

Now let's talk about the reasons why some *products* in a catalog do much better than others, and how you can reduce your risks by using some prescreening techniques.

Naturally, the best way to find out about a product is to test it. But the fixed cost of preparation, especially if you are using color, is high. In addition, if you can knock out a few items from the test mode, you are making room for others that may have a better chance of success.

Let's look at some of these factors that make for a good or bad selection.

1. *The product matches your theme.* Each catalog should have a theme or direction to its merchandise selection. As we said earlier, that theme matches certain types of mailing lists, or certain types of magazine subscribers. When you depart from this theme, you greatly reduce the chance your *customers* will respond.

2. *The product varies from your price or quality range.* Surprisingly, you can often go up in price. As you go up, the amount available to cover your catalog or promotion cost is greater. Customers can be sold up too.

Our terminology for "price range" really comes down to similar *quality.* You certainly can sell a $3 apple corer to a $200 food processor customer. But, it had better be a *quality* apple corer.

It is very difficult to sell down. There are lots of reasons that make it almost impossible to sell down. People's tastes, as they get older, go up. Psychologically, people prefer buying less but maintaining or increasing their standards.

Perhaps the most compelling reason lies in the numbers. When you go down in price, you have fewer products available for catalog or promotion. That is why gift and gadget catalogs went out of business.

3. *Universality of appeal.* The more readers of your catalog or ad that could be interested in your product, the greater chance for sales.

This is the main impetus for items selected as traffic builders—those items offered in small space ads to hook you as a customer. For example, more people will buy a set of mixing bowls than apple corers. Everyone can use mixing bowls. Not everybody likes apples or has any need to core them.

4. *Perceived to be hard to find.* Imports do well because the reader perceives they are not generally available. It increases sales when you state "imported" or "exclusive." Then, too, people like to feel they have something that not everyone else has. A French apple corer might sell better than just an apple corer.

5. *The product will be as pictured and described.* When one can't see, feel, or touch the product they are buying, the seller has the problem of acceptability. People are wary of what they don't know about. If the product is well known, there is usually

no problem. If it is not familiar, it could be a big stumbling block. An apple corer is an apple corer. But, what is a croque monsieur?

As an illustration, it is easier to know and accept what you are getting with something like a pair of scissors than how a child's outfit, pictured on a four-year-old, will look on a six-year-old, or how a dress on a blonde would look on a brunette.

6. *There are no apprehensions about sizes or colors.* The greatest apparel successes in mail order are the "one size fits all" products—wrap-arounds, muumuus, and so on. As soon as you go into sizes, you have to stock a lot more merchandise. That costs money and increases risk.

The problem holds true with colors. To remove the apprehension that the one color won't look right, catalogers add color choices. That means added inventory, and the additional problem that after the promotion listing the sales, you may have too much of one color left and just enough of the other color to be too skimpy to advertise. This means you could possibly face expensive out-of-stock fulfillment and reply costs.

7. *Perceive heavy utilization.* People are naturally thrifty. If they perceive that something is very useful, or that the gift will be well received, they have a greater tendency to purchase.

It becomes necessary for the copywriter to state alternate uses of products—to build up the confidence that it will be used, and used a great deal.

Because of the guilt complex which often arises when a member of the family buys something for themselves, it is important to point out how other family members will also use and enjoy it.

8. *It's all I need to buy.* People don't like future obligations when they purchase something. They want the assurance that they will have no further obligations after the initial sale. If I purchase the glassware, then will I need new tableware? Will the

blouse go with what I have, or must I also buy a skirt and accessories? Copy must give confidence that the item, by itself, is just what the reader wishes.

9. *The product is in the early stages of a fad.* There is nothing more dangerous than faddish or trendy products. Women's apparel is the most dangerous area. That is why products that continue to be in style, like tennis clothes, do well in catalogs.

High-tech products can be dangerous because they are soon superseded by products with newer bells and whistles, or the same thing at a lower price.

If you have a fad product, you have a double problem. You can be too early, so no one knows about it, or you can be too late and miss the action.

10. *The product will not become worthless shortly.* Products that relate to political conventions die a quick death. Calendars are hard to sell after January 1st. Holly wreaths are hard to sell after Christmas, as are hearts after Valentine's Day, or candy eggs after Easter. Other examples are children's clothes or toys that are quickly outgrown.

11. *The product is oversold.* If you promise too much, the recipient will be disappointed. The result will be a returned product, and perhaps a person with a bad taste in their mouth—not a future prospect to become a customer.

12. *The product is not widely available at retail.* Obvious examples are products that are available where you have to shop on a frequent basis, like anything sold in a grocery store. Mass merchandisers can usually sell cheaper than mail order, so you are behind the eight-ball before you start.

It would be easy to say that products not generally found in stores would be best. However, if it is not available in any kind of store, it may be because no one wants it!

Packaging, especially gift packaging, can often offset the problem of widespread availability. Many stores won't giftwrap and ship, or don't do it with the quality the customer desires.

There is something special about receiving a case of grapefruit directly from Texas, even though you could have purchased the same grapefruit at your local grocery store. If you can build up an image, you may capture retail business lacking that image.

There are undoubtedly many more of these danger or screening areas. It is a good idea to put your products against them and see if they pass the test. Not only will this prescreen undesirable selections, but it will also lead you to ideas on alternate products that may have a better chance for success.

PICKING THE RIGHT MAIL ORDER ITEMS

If you are thinking about going into mail order, a five minute test may save your life savings. Most people who go into mail order shouldn't. In fact, less than one in twenty we see receives a recommendation from us to proceed. This quick test is designed to quickly weed out at least 15 of the 20 mailers that shouldn't waste any more of their time on that project.

Rule 1. Just because your spouse likes it,
doesn't mean it will sell.

In mail order, it is the mass market that counts. If you can't quickly relate to the small town prospect in mid-America, you shouldn't be making judgment. I've got a formula that works for me. If I like it, it won't sell.

What does sell? That is hard to answer. One clue might help. Don't look at the product. Look at the ad that will be used to sell that product. Will it sound exciting; provide a basic benefit? Mail order is the opposite of retail. Judge the ad, not the product, as the decision to buy will be made before the product is ever seen.

Rule 2. A four-time mark-up is not enough.

A four-time mark-up means you sell it for four times your cost. Some products, especially books, can survive on four times. But, because you've probably forgotten some costs, stick with five times.

Rule 3. Beat the competition's lowest price.

It is true you don't have to *always* be the lowest price. But mail order prices on hot items tend to go down, not up—double digit inflation notwithstanding. The chances are that by the time you get launched, prices will come down.

Rule 4. Plan what you are going to sell to your customer next.

Other than in publishing, what mail order successes do you know of that have made it on just one product? Very few. Would you believe that most mail order space advertising you see is designed to capture you as a customer at a loss? They will make it up on a catalog of products or reorders that they will sell you in the future. That is why you see so many catalogs and not many single items.

The whole mail order world builds around your customer list. You may get 5–10–20 times the response from your customers over cold prospects. It is inexpensive to advertise to your customers and expensive to prospects. To make money over the long pull, you'd better be able to sell again and again to your customers.

Rule 5. You will go broke under $19.95.

Maybe an exaggeration! We think not. Low ticket (priced) items, even with a good mark-up, don't have enough allowance for advertising and overhead. For example, if your advertising budget is 50% of selling price, you've got $1.00 for advertising on a $2.00 item—but almost $10.00 on a $19.95 item. You must sell an awful lot of $2.00 items to cover your advertising costs.

Rule 6. Find a market you can reach inexpensively.

If you have a product that appeals to people who have no unifying profile, you will have a hard time finding them. For example, you may have the most wonderful recipe for raspberry jam. But how do you isolate people who really like raspberry jam? On the other hand, if you're selling a new swimming pool cleaning device in Southern California, you can obtain a mailing list of every swimming pool owner in Southern California. Every person you advertise to is a potential customer.

A wise mail order expert once said: "It is better to select an audience and fit mail order products to it than to find a product and fit an audience to it." There are many catalogs that have done just that: cooking products, sewing products, unusual carpentry tools, to name a few.

If you can pass all these rules, your pot of gold may be nearer than you think.

SIX

AUDIENCE

WHY DIRECT MAIL COSTS SO MUCH MORE—AND WORKS

The high cost of direct mail and telephone is a function of technology. Why they work and are cost efficient is a function of audience.

Broadly speaking, some people are good prospects and some people are not prospects at all. To separate them is important. Let's take an example: If you are selling caviar and only one person in ten thousand likes caviar, can afford caviar, and is ready to buy *now*, there is no reason to advertise to the other 9999.

Targeted media aren't perfect. But, it can properly define one out of 50 people mailed who would buy. That is the difference between mass media and targeted media.

Mass media, radio, television, newspapers, and consumer magazines say: "Buy me. I'm so cheap that you will find your caviar buyers among my large circulation."

Targeted media, direct mail, and telephone say: "We will deliver you your caviar buyers because we can target directly to them."

Sure, this targeting isn't perfect. It cuts out a lot of waste audience—but one, two, five, maybe ten out of one hundred are ready to buy. But because direct mail can tell a longer story, and phone can be more persuasive, they become efficient.

The science of figuring this all out is the science of media, or audience selection. As many people-hours are put into this area as the highly visible creative area, and their efforts can be *more* productive.

The best message to the wrong audience is worthless. The worst message to the right audience will get you some business. Obviously, direct mail and telephone are only used when the right audience is available.

Your Customer—the Right Audience

The best audience is your customers. They already know you; they know your product or service; they have confidence in you; they have an interest or need in what you sell.

Direct mail or telephone work best to present customers. That fact has lead to the Data Base Revolution, which simply means every customer must be captured and converted into a firm's data base. The constant use of that data base to get more business from these past customers is the most efficient advertising or promotion an organization can do.

Direct mail and telephone work because they have these targeted data bases to start with. Reorders for office products, magazine subscription renewal programs, catalogs to customers, new services for utilities, new financial services for bank customers, insurance policy renewals, and large donor renewals all work with direct mail because the audience is targeted. Membership renewals, product reordering and replenishing, warranty renewals, and insurance renewals all work for marketing because of their extremely targeted nature. Lists closely related to past customer lists may also be successful. These would include catalog inquiries, magazine subscription expirations, requests for more information, and customer lists of competitors. These work because *it is known* the person has already expressed an interest in what you are offering.

Wasted Audiences

Of all the factors we have discussed that relate to waste audience, geographical waste is one of the most prevalent and the most media related.

If I'm mailing to owners of butcher shops in Southern California, there are, according to the Yellow Pages, about 220. Why advertise in the metropolitan paper, with circulation in excess of one million, if I am only trying to reach 220 and I know who the 220 are. The same problem occurs with television and radio. Plus, how many of the 220 butcher shop owners will read the paper the day I advertise, or will see my TV commercial, or hear my radio commercial? At least with direct mail they will glance at my envelope or have an opportunity to turn down my phone call.

The entire advertising industry is dedicated to doing a better job of targeting. This is true for mass media just as much as targeted media.

WHY MAIL GLUT IS A FALLACY

Direct mail professionals are getting a larger share of prospects' and customers' attention and, therefore, more than their share of business, because they recognize a little-known fact that should

be as plain as the nose on any advertiser's face: *most people receive only a fraction of the mail everybody thinks they do.* Smart
advertisers are using this fact to great advantage when budgeting
their media mix for campaigns to consumers or businesses.

Most advertising people believe, by the flood of mail *they* receive, that the world is flooded with junk mail. In fact, the exact
opposite is true. A definitive United States Postal Service study
shows that the *average household receives less than three pieces* of
advertising mail a day. Much less mail is received than is generally
thought.

Category	Pieces per Week
First Class	7.6
Second Class	2.1
Third Class, Advertising	3.3
Third Class, Non-Profit	1.1

One reason for the misconception is that people in advertising
receive much more mail than people in any other industry.

My own checkered career is a good example. When I first
worked in advertising agencies, my mountain of mail was almost
insurmountable. After a switch to a client position in advertising,
it dropped at least 50%. A further switch, to president of a line
operation, dropped it another 50%.

There may be a glut among those people who donate or purchase by mail. Why? These people are on more mailing lists as
customers and donors. As we have said before, there is a higher
response rate from mail responsive names, so their names get
mailed more often. They simply work better.

Even if a good mail respondent gets as many as 10 or 20 pieces
of mail a day, that doesn't mean a mail glut to that person. That
person is responding enough to make mailing to him or her prof-

itable. Heavy responders must be used to receiving lots of mail or they wouldn't be heavy responders.

So, you see, glut doesn't really happen. The glut level varies by person. Glut seeks its own level, because if a person who responds well receives a great deal of mail, then their response rate per mailer will drop, and over a period of time less mail will be directed to that person.

A better definition of glut would be too much mail for a particular person to respond to—so, that person responds less and becomes an unprofitable name for mailers. You don't have glut until response rates drop.

For a person who never buys or donates by mail, one piece of mail is a glut. For a heavy mail order buyer and contributor, 10 pieces a day may not even be a glut.

Another glut situation appears when a person gets too much mail in categories for which there is absolutely no interest. For example, let's take a relatively high income zip code. Assume that there is a very small low-income segment in that zip code—not enough to drag down its overall high income rating. Mailers with high income products and services would mail that zip code frequently. The low income segment would be glutted with mail because the high income products would not be appealing to them, or affordable.

Glut is reduced by the mail order industry continually developing better ways to target mail to likely prospects. Glut occurs when mail misses its target.

WHY MAILING MORE FREQUENTLY DOES NOT HURT RESULTS

If you are in fund-raising, your prospect is ready to give to something every six weeks. If you are selling merchandise, remember that the big companies mail to their best customers up to 50 times a year. Why does this frequency help rather than hinder?

The answer lies in studying the prospect, customer, or donor. You've got to look at the opportunity from their point of view.

Fund-raising is the easiest to explain. Your prospect probably goes to church each week and supports the collection plate. So, it is safe to say that most people give to a charitable cause at least once a week. That is 52 times a year.

From that point of view, giving on an average of every six weeks doesn't sound out of reason. The point is, somebody is ready to give to somebody more frequently than you think. It might as well be you.

The older we get, the more we give. The more we feel that our days and years are numbered and wonder if we have done our fair share, the more we give. The more frequently we are asked and the more we are reminded of our responsibilities, the more we give.

Many large fund-raising mailers have worried about the possibility of increased mailings having a negative effect on a total year's giving or on long-range giving. Test after test proves frequency helps, not hurts, total programs.

The commercial world must be approached differently. Several factors come into play simultaneously. I'm offered *what* I want to buy; I'm offered *when* I want to buy it; it has not been offered to me from *other sources* more attractively; I am offered it when I can *afford* it; I liked it so much, I want *more*; I need *replenishment*. These factors are all self-explanatory. But, there is another factor that must overlay all of these. I am subject to other advertising about your product or service from other sources. The dripping water slowly takes effect and I finally decide to buy. If your offer reaches me at that particular time, I'm going to buy from you. At any given moment of time, enough people you've reached are at that point to give *you* the response you need.

We should not mix up two different facets of this phenomenon. My mail box is too full because I'm receiving mail from so many different places, versus my mail box is too full because I'm hearing from you too often. I've not seen tests on this, but common sense dictates that the former case is far more common than the latter.

Some wise person once defined junk mail as advertising mail you had no interest in. Prove it to yourself. Think of your favorite catalog. What if you received a new and different one twice as often as you now do? Wouldn't you read it? If you read it, there is a good chance you will buy from it.

One final note on frequency. Here are two ways to do it. Repeat what you are doing exactly the same way, or tell the story from a different point each mailing. Either can be successful. It is important to test and keep track to determine what works best for you.

In catalogs, most successful mailers find they can mail their fall holiday gift catalog *twice*, by just changing the cover. Readers will not remember receiving the previous one and will read it through, although the inside pages are the same, and will purchase at a profitable rate—often a better rate of response than an inquiry list mailing. This success happens because your catalog was there when the prospect was ready to act. Perhaps your previous catalog caused them to almost buy. This time they couldn't resist the temptation.

No discussion of frequency would be complete without referring to "X" dates. In business mail and insurance mail there are what we call "X" dates, or expiration dates. That is the date their present insurance is to expire, and the only time a prospect would consider changing his program of insurance. Unfortunately, the "X" dates are usually unavailable on mailing lists. Enough mailings must be made to cover the entire year so that at least one mailing arrives close enough to an expiration date and the new offer is given consideration.

Fortunately, frequency can be easily tested to find the right frequency for you.

TARGETING THE DECISION MAKER

Not long ago, a new client in a high-technology field was moaning that she had less than 1000 firms that could use her product. Of course, her product sold for over $100,000 and a five percent share of market would be over $5 million in sales.

She was ready to throw us out when we recommended that she mail 10,000 pieces of mail, quite a bit more than the 700 pieces she was planning on mailing. These would be directed to several influencers in each of the 700+ companies on her list. After this explanation, it all made sense.

You Are Never Talking to the Decision Maker

. . . unless there is only one employee in the company!

There are two kinds of customers in this world—those who don't like to make decisions, and either do nothing or ask others; or, there are those who make decisions, but first ask others for input to make the best possible decision. Note that in either case, others are asked. So, there is always more than one person involved in making a decision.

I once had a boss who was president of a billion dollar corporation and known for his quick and decisive decisions. After working with him for a while, I found he was even smarter than I'd thought. He would quickly get input from outside members of his board or other peers and then make a quick decision. Even here, influencers were far more important than the business community realized.

Five Types of Influencers Who Affect Decisions

Here is why, especially on high-ticket items, you should mail to more than one person in a prospect organization. There are several types of influencers who affect decisions.

1. *The person who needs the product.*   This is probably the person you are already talking to. Obviously, this individual is interested in making the job easier, improving quality, capability, and so on. But rarely is this person the decision maker—only an influencer, even in his or her own area.

2. *The operating or line supervisor.*   That is the next level up. They will obviously be direct beneficiaries of better productivity from within the operation.

3. *The financial officer.*   A professional who is extremely proficient in saying "no!" This person rarely speaks, much less understands, the technical language of the technical section of the organization.

4. *The chief operating officer.*   The president gets in on an unbelievable number of decisions, especially those involved with spending money. Sometimes the president doesn't speak the same technical language either.

5. *The research and development chief.*   Here the opportunity is not so much to reach a decision influencer, but to communicate that your product or service does exist. This person could be more valuable than anyone because months later they might have uncovered a new use for your product or service.

Why Mail All These Influencers?

There are several good reasons to mail to all these influencers.

1. *No salesperson can reach them all.* Most people will not share who the real decision influencers are. They like to give the feeling that they are the decision makers, but they are not.

2. *The person who needs the item is usually a poor communicator.* Technical people are known for their difficulty in communicating to nontechnical people. You can usually communicate your story better to the influencers.

3. *Influencers can be instigators.* Directions of companies often change and people down the line are not yet aware. I remember once, as a corporate staff officer, walking into a line department head's office and saying, "Don't you think we should computerize this function?" The department head was speechless, having no idea the company would ever entertain such an idea, even though it had been on his mind for over a year.

4. *The barrier of technical language.* The nontechnical branch of the company will often give the impression they understand more than they do. If you communicate directly, and express what you have to say in universally understood language regarding how you meet their needs, you have dramatically improved your chances of making the sale.

Now we have taken our 1000 main prospects and mailed to five different titles. That is 5000 pieces of mail. What about our other 5000 pieces?

Why not mail to the conceptualists in companies *outside your known* customer list? See how many of these Research & Development types find new applications that no one in your organization ever thought of. It could get you into industries entirely new to your operation.

10× Mailing Quantity for 2× Cost

We have increased our mailing size tenfold—for only two times the cost. What a bargain. Your creative development and production costs went against the first 1000 pieces and were the same no matter how many pieces were mailed. The extra 9000 pieces were an incremental paper and printing cost. Nine times more pieces for only twice the cost!

THE SEASONALITY MYTH

Mail during summer? Why not! Mail at Christmas time? Why not! Mail at tax time? Why not!

The public is telling us with increasing frequency that it doesn't make any difference if *certain principles are followed.*

Common Sense Destroys Mailing Myths

As we all know, the best way to decide anything about marketing is to put yourself in the prospect's shoes. Let's then use common sense to destroy some myths and generate some extra profits while the competition isn't looking.

1. *The trend is to year-round vacations.* Skiing in winter and traveling when tourist havens are not summer-crowded and when there are fewer families with children (especially marketing decision-makers), combine to even out vacations and make summer no different from the other seasons.

2. *Nonsummer and non-Christmas periods are peak business travel periods.* If you are mailing to business, there are more conventions, trade shows, seminars, business meetings, and sales meetings in spring, winter, and fall than in summer. Thus, if you

mail in those traditionally popular mailing months, you may find your prospect away more often!

3. *Tax times may be the best times.* More and more prospects are paying quarterly taxes. At the traditional April 15th time they may be getting a refund! For many others, year-round withholding covers the tax. In business mail, most of your prospects aren't involved with corporate tax mailers. We've had several mailers who had delays and found themselves mailing at tax time. Each time the mailings have been successful. Many people are mailing their returns early, so by April 15th they've forgotten their tax problems.

4. *There is less competition during traditional slow mailing periods.* If 10% of the prospect audience is on vacation, but 10% less competitive mailings go out, it's a wash!

5. *People are shopping earlier.* Who even thought of mailing a Christmas gift catalog in August? Now almost everyone does.

6. *People are shopping by mail later.* The advent of ordering by telephone has opened up last-minute shopping, especially when there is a pleasant voice on the other end, reassuring timely delivery.

So now we've taken off all the blinders. You can mail *anytime*. Yes, even at Christmas.

When Should You Mail?

Again, common sense dictates. Let's put together a checklist that can apply to both business and residential mail.

1. *Mail when your product or service is needed.* You can't sell snowshoes in June. You can't sell me insurance when my present policy has eight more months before my next annual premium is due.

Spend more time thinking: When do my prospects need my product or service? If you are selling insurance for homes or autos, you can be fairly certain that the "X" date, or expiration date, is close to the anniversary of the date of purchase.

2. *Mail ahead of the need.* Too many mailers follow retail promotion schedules. Retail can deliver instantly. Purchase by mail takes a while. Plus, consumers don't take chances. They order way ahead, maybe two months, so they are certain what they order will arrive on time. Two months is a good time lead, with three months at Christmas, because everyone is after the "gift" dollar.

3. *Test mailing when competition doesn't.* This concept goes against one of the rules I have stressed: Follow what others do over and over again. But we should be looking for some new holes in the marketplace. Offbeat timing could be such a hole and be lucrative. All prospects don't march to the same drum.

4. *Don't mail all at once.* It gets cold (or warm) at different times in different parts of the country. Hunting and fishing seasons vary by stage (and targets!). Rainy and planting seasons vary. Try breaking your mailings down to time of need.

5. *Follow your customers' hints.* If you are in gift mail order and you have customers who buy in November and others who buy in September, you'd better get your catalog to them when they want to buy.

6. *Make off-season promotions pay.* Summer clearance of skis may move a lot of skis. We are finding that people are hedging inflation by taking a deal *now*.

When in doubt, remember: It is not when you have to sell, it is when the customer (or prospect) wants to buy. When should you mail? Ask them! Listen to them!

WHY PROFESSIONALS DO NOT GUESS RESPONSE RATES

Here is a good way to evaluate the degree of direct mail order expertise of someone you are consulting. Ask them what response you might expect for your new project. If they answer the question with a figure, you can be sure you are talking to someone who knows very *little* about direct response advertising. Take their reply with a grain of salt. Then get to work and dig out some meaningful figures yourself about response rates. The truth is you can only get a good handle on response rates by testing.

Would a doctor give you a date your tennis elbow pain will go away? Will a lawyer indicate what the jury will do? In all cases, the reason for not being able to answer is the same—there are too many factors involved to give a meaningful reply.

Dozens of factors affect mailing and coupon results. Some of the important ones are likely to be: price, uniqueness of product, competition's price, penetration of competition's advertising, ability to select lists, creative approach, guarantee statement, seasons, the image of the mailer, and most important these days, economic conditions.

You still need an answer. How does one go about preparing a budget or pro forma to set monetary needs to start in mail order, or set a business lead budget? One way to do it is to budget breakeven response rates and work backwards. Then you will at least know where you are as you go along. If you have a bench mark, and your project should be aborted quickly, you'll know it quickly.

Using a hypothetical example, allow 50% of sales for promotion, product costs of $10, and selling price of $20. The finer points—returns, no-pays, shipping charges, and so on—can all be refined later. At what response rate will you break even? First, figure out your advertising (mailing) or acquisition cost. Assume it is $300 per thousand. This may be difficult to estimate, as your mailing quantity is a key factor in estimating costs. For now, pick a printing quantity that you think may be reasonable and start with it. You can adjust it later, if necessary.

Use this formula to get the number of orders or responses at break-even: Mailing cost per thousand divided by the net of unit selling price less unit cost. If your mailing cost is $300 per thousand, your product sells for $20, and its cost is $10, then you have $10 for advertising and promotion, based upon the 50% formula described above. You must get 30 orders to break even ($300 per thousand divided by $10 = 30 orders per thousand to break even).

You can use this formula to solve break-even response rates—maximum allowable for mailing costs at break-even, or break-even price.

Here is how you can use this same formula to establish minimum selling price. Using our example above, let's now expect a 1% response rate. What is the lowest price we can sell at and still break even?

A 1% response rate is 10 orders per thousand. Divide the 10 orders into the advertising cost per thousand (in our case, $300 per thousand) and your fixed advertising cost per sale is $30. Add that to your product cost ($10) and you must sell the product at $40 to break even—before bad pays, returns, overhead, and profit. Add these and compare your selling price to the market. Are you in the ball park?

See how important putting the pencil to paper is!

WHY NAMES ARE NOT STOLEN
Don't Worry About Theft

At least once a week somebody says to me, "I'd be afraid to rent my mailing list—somebody might steal it."

There are two fallacies to that statement. First, not many people will think your list is as valuable as you do. Secondly, there are very easy ways to prevent your list from being misused. In over 4000 mailing list rentals, I never once saw the misuse of a mailing list. It just doesn't happen. The few cases I've heard of were the results of naiveté or ignorance of people new to the business.

Renting Your List

When you rent your mailing list to others, it can be a large source of income. We know of mail order companies who make their entire profit from the rental of their mailing list, not from the merchandise they sell. It's not uncommon to make over $100,000 a year from a mailing list. There are some 30,000 mailing lists on the market, and the right list, working for the right person, can be a well-worth-it expense. So, seriously consider renting your mailing list.

If it's a small list, under 25,000 or 50,000 names, there are probably not very many people who will be interested in it. When you get over 100,000 names, your list becomes meaningful and can be marketed successfully.

If you want to make sure your list isn't misused, you should do what most mailers do. They put special names and addresses in their file, maybe their own name slightly misspelled, with a different first name. These are called "dummy" names. Doing this is called "salting the list." When the firm renting your list receives it, they have no way to know which names are dummy names. They usually mail the whole list, so your dummy gets mailed. When you receive your dummy names back, you compare it against your order and see if anybody has used your list without authorization. It's kind of like balancing your checkbook every month. It's rare that the bank makes a mistake, but it's something you do anyway.

Trading Names

Trading names is becoming more popular with people who mail. It works like this. You give me 20,000 of your names and I'll give you 20,000 of mine. This eliminates the cost of renting a mailing list—a cost that usually runs between $30 and $50 per thousand names rented.

When *not* to rent your list: There are certain times when it's probably not to your advantage to rent your mailing list. One is a situation where you're not comfortable with the ethics of the offer going out using your list. If you have the slightest doubt in this area, do not rent your names. Remember, you have the right to review all mailing packages *before* you authorize your list to be used. Be sure the mailing package you review is the one that is going to be used with your names.

It's probably wise not to trade names or to rent your names to direct competitors—people who are in the same exact business you are. Notice I said same *exact* business. It's quite acceptable, if you're in a category selling high end merchandise, to rent your names to somebody who's selling low end merchandise of the same kind. If you do decide to rent to your competitors, be sure that they don't mail ahead of or at the same time you do. Get your mailing out *before* you permit them to mail your names— so their prospect and your customer has *your* mailing first.

What about invasion of privacy? You've heard a lot of talk about people being upset about their name being on a mailing list. It's a small but vocal minority. The Direct Mail Marketing Association continues to offer, through ads in various magazines, the opportunity for the public to have their names either taken off of mailing lists or added on. The readership of these ads exceeds many millions. The result: The number of people who want their names added to mailing lists is over twice as large as those who want their names taken off! Less than 1/10 of 1% want their names taken off of mailing lists.

If you are a mailer and you do rent your list, be sure to put a disclaimer in your mailing catalog or mailing package stating that names are rented to a select number of firms. If you write the Direct Mail Marketing Association, 6 East 43rd Street, New York, New York, 10017, they will send you samples of ways to state this disclaimer unobtrusively. It can be a sentence as simple as: "From time to time, we offer merchandise and services from others. If you do not wish to receive such mailings from others, please send us your name and address."

The Presidential Commission on Privacy has reviewed the direct mail list industry very carefully. They came to the conclusion that there was no harm done by the rental of mailing lists to others. They did suggest, however, that people should have the right to have their name removed, if they so desire.

Income from mailing list rentals is bottom line money. Are you getting yours?

WHY THIRD CLASS MAIL WORKS AS WELL AS FIRST CLASS

Perhaps as much money is wasted mailing First Class rather than Third Class as in any other area of direct mail. That wastage is due to a misunderstanding of what the real differences are.

To put the problem in perspective, we must remember "works as well" means "works as well per dollar spent." Let us say our mailing package costs $500 per thousand pieces mailed, including

First Class postage of 20¢ or $200 per thousand. Third Class postage is 11¢ or $110 per thousand. The cost of mailing at Third Class is $410 per thousand. That is a savings of 18%. Thus, a response rate that drops anything less than 18% with the lower postage is more efficient.

In our discussion we must also assume that the mailing is not going out late and has a deadline for response. In that case, it must be First Class or don't mail.

Mailers who try to gauge mail to arrive a certain day of the week, anywhere except the post office they mailed from, are kidding themselves. I cannot think of a reason to receive mail a certain day of the week. Many people don't read mail daily because, quite simply, they are either not there or have higher priorities for their time.

Proper planning can control the arrival of Third Class mail within a week, almost anywhere in the United States, except, perhaps, during the Christmas season.

One of the main reasons people new to direct marketing shy away from Third Class mail is that they feel Third Class mail will be perceived as junk mail, while First Class won't.

This is, in a large part, a misconception because junk mail is only junk if it has no appeal to the reader.

Mailers frequently use metered mail for Third Class mail. It takes a close inspection of the metered area to see if the piece went Third or First Class. Most people don't bother to look.

Will Third Class business mail get past a secretary? Barring a blanket order of "I don't want to see any junk mail," Third Class mail does get through if it is done correctly. Quality of stationery or typed address rather than a label address, have much more to do with it than the postage, if metered. (There is a Third Class precancelled postage stamp you can use if you are really worried about appearance.)

If you have a label address and a First Class stamp, the label may do more damage to appearance than the postage rate does good.

The cost of metered mail or affixing a precancelled stamp is minimal because the mail usually goes through the same machine that must seal the envelope.

About 95% of the advertising mail our organization produces goes out Third Class.

If you still insist on going First Class, you should consider printing the words "FIRST CLASS MAIL" on the envelope to make sure the reader knows you've spent the extra money.

Because so many people now respond to or buy by mail, its stigma has been erased. A survey of large corporations reported that over half of all its office managers had responded by mail to an offer within the past six months.

It used to be that the class of mail indicated its importance. Telegrams were first, then Air Mail, then First Class, and finally Third Class. Now it is by interest of the recipient to the product or service offered.

WHY SOME LISTS WORK BETTER THAN OTHERS

There must be over 30 or 40 thousand different lists you could choose from. Some work better than others. Why?

The Mail Order Characteristic

The mail order characteristic, or the respond-to-mail characteristic, varies widely by *individual*, not by company. Some people absolutely refuse to read junk mail. Others read it for fun but never respond. Others will respond to some types of offers, but not other types. There is an increasing number that will respond if the offer is interesting. With them, the fact that it came by mail is no hurdle.

People who respond to something by mail are more apt to respond to something else by mail. These people are called mail order responders. They are the customers of someone who sells by mail. There is a better chance they will respond to you than non-mail order respondents. In fact, it often happens that the fact they respond to mail is a more important selection criteria than any other factor.

The problem is that there are not enough of them when you overlay other requirements, such as: age, have children, are in a certain business classification, or give to charity. So you have to look carefully at other criteria.

Magazine Subscribers

A big source for names is the subscriber lists of most magazines. Large quantities of such lists are often found. They relate to what you are selling because they read *Money, House & Garden, Popular Mechanics, Architectural Digest, Iron Age,* or *Advertising Age.* The list is endless because most magazines rent out their subscriber lists.

By and large, they don't work as well as mail responders because a magazine subscription does not reveal mail buying habits.

Some magazines segment their list so you can rent only the subscribers who responded to a mail subscription offer from that publication. That means you don't have to rent and mail those people who received the magazine as a gift, or who subscribed from a reply card within the magazine.

Following the pattern we have discussed, the mail subscribers seem to always pull better than the non-mail subscribers.

But even the mail subscribers don't respond as well as most response lists (mail order buyers of products and services, *not* magazine subscribers) because about the only way to subscribe to a magazine is from a mail offer.

Directory Lists—Consumer

The big size lists are the directory lists or demographic lists. The largest lists are all the households in the nation and most of the car owners (some states do not make car owner lists available). There are also lists by telephone number.

There are all kinds of specialty lists too. These would include lists of college students, high school students, teachers, names from social registers, alumni, political party members, airline passengers, warranty card replies, and many more.

These lists do not work as well as subscriber-by-mail lists, and definitely not as well as response lists. Again, the reason is that nothing is known about the mail order buying habits.

Directory Lists—Business

Unfortunately, there are few large response lists available for business that can be categorized to a business group. The reason for this is the fact that most of these lists are small and much of the business-to-business list business is offering information, rather than selling something.

It is just as true that these directory based lists don't respond as well as response lists.

Notice that in this business list discussion I have left out subscription lists. The reason is that business lists are tricky in that many of them, especially those who offer lists, are controlled circulation publications. That means they are given away free to business people. Thus they cannot qualify as mail respondents because the response did not require payment.

Another reason magazines have been omitted is that the name of the person subscribing is often suspect because the renewal comes to the same name, even though the person who subscribed may be in another department of the organization.

The big business lists are based on a compilation of telephone Yellow Page listings or credit reports. They are successfully used because so much of the business mail is lead generating, rather than mail order.

Fund-Raising

Fund-raising list principles follow the same pattern. Donors to one cause are more likely to give to another cause. More specifically, contributors who responded to a mail solicitation will respond to someone else's mail solicitation.

In fact, there is a good correlation of people who respond to a mail product offer, such as a catalog, also responding very well to fund-raising solicitations. Again, it comes down to the point that increasing response to mail means a better prospect.

How to Determine Better Mail Responders

Just how do you find those who respond to mail more often? These people appear on more mailing lists you can rent. By merging lists together, you find "hits," which is when the same name is found on another list. These multiple responders are better prospects.

Another way to find better prospects is by mailing *newer* names. These newer names are called "hotline" names. Newer names respond better because they are less apt to have moved. A less tangible reason, and one that requires much further study, is that at certain times people are more apt to buy by mail than at other times. Such times are when they move, get married, have children, or go away to school. Changing jobs is probably another factor, but this is hard to get data on. Changing jobs naturally relates to the moving factor too.

Another signal for better responders is *how much* they buy by mail. This monetary category applies to goods and services and fund-raising. The larger the purchase or donation, the better the prospect—not only that they may spend or donate more, but also that they tend to do it *more often*.

Frequency of purchase or donation is a similar positive factor. The more often you respond to a mail offer or solicitation, the better prospect you are.

I've said little about the obvious reason—buying something by mail that is *similar* to what you are offering is a big factor. It needs no explanation.

Remembering these principles will help you decide if your idea is good enough to be successful in mail order, because enough lists are available and give you a basis for better selection in the future.

WHY YOU CAN OFTEN FIND THE LIST YOU CANNOT FIND

Your products are certificates of deposit, stocks and bonds. You really need a list of wealthy people who are into stocks, bonds, and other financial instruments. The problem is that there are no lists that isolate the people with significant liquid assets. You have to find another way.

The best way is to contact a vendor. Use a mailing list broker if you are offering products or seeking funds from the general public. Use list compilers as contacts when you plan to use a business list or are going to a wide range of customers. The difference between brokers and compilers is described elsewhere in this book.

You run a risk when you go to list owners because they will often push their own list, rather than be objective. They will show you how to segment their list. It will be a way, but not necessarily the best way. Before you seek a broker or vendor, you should do some investigating yourself. This not only makes you more knowledgeable, but you may find something even the experts hadn't thought of.

The first step to finding a good answer is to profile your market. If you already have customers, determine what their unique characteristics are, and which ones can be reasonably grouped together to represent the entire body. How old? What do they read? Are they male or female? And so on.

Next match your profile against the norm and see where they differ. Look for the skew or difference. It may be that people who have lived in the same house for more than 10 years are better prospects. When you find that skew (for example, old-time residents are found to pull twice as well as a general list), then go to the next step.

What other characteristics represent this skewed factor? In our illustration, do those long-time residents own their home or rent? Are they families or simple heads of households? What is their age?

Next let's go back to our first example, the search for people with assets. Maybe you find that many of them subscribe to *Forbes* magazine, are over 50 years old, or contribute to conservative causes. If so, you now know what characteristics you need to find in the lists you are considering testing.

If these answers are not readily available, the next step is to put yourself in your customer's shoes. What would you then buy, contribute to, or donate to?

By the way, you can cross over between buyers and donors. In testing some fifty lists for a museum, we found the best list was charge account customers for a major conservative men's clothing chain. We happened upon this list at a cocktail party at the museum, because we thought and speculated what the group had in common. We thought of where they might purchase their clothes.

If you are still having a hard time deducing what lists might be best, you may wish to contact a noncompetitive organization. For a museum, you can contact similar museums in other cities and ask them what they use successfully. You will be pleasantly surprised how quickly and positively they will answer, especially if you limit the questions to four or less and enclose a self-addressed, stamped envelope.

If you are still stuck, you probably shouldn't use mailing lists at all but rather go to a two-step prospecting operation. Run an ad with a strongly related offer, or offer the most universal item in your catalog. Those people who are truly interested will respond and allow you to build your own mailing list.

To get the maximum number of responses, offer something free. It obviously has to relate to what you are really selling or you will get poor prospects to identify themselves.

In our illustration of seeking people with sufficient assets to purchase certificates of deposit, stocks, or bonds, the offer could well be: "How To Find Tax Loopholes in Stock and Bond Taxation Laws." Anyone responding to that offer must have liquid assets to invest.

The use of paper products as the offer usually makes sense. Booklets going right to the subject matter can be written in little time and the direct marketing promotional effort for them is comparatively simple.

Remember that response lists are someone's customer list. Also remember that a directory of any size has undoubtedly been converted to tape and is available in label form for list rental purposes.

Much of list success is from the proper segmentation within a list. If you have a list that looks marginally good, you might be able to segment such a list and make it work well for you.

There are many combinations of lists. The incumbent advertising agency should keep on top of the problems or opportunities to assure that every reasonable factor has been tried.

Some unusual selections are expressed here, simply to show how this thinking process works. Here is an example.

An airline wanted to beef up one route. A list was found of businesses at point A with headquarters at one end of point A of the route, and branch facilities at the other, point B. The specifications were then reversed, seeking those additional companies with headquarters at point B and branches at point A.

Creativity is not limited to the copy and graphics for your program. Media or list creativity is even more important, and should make a bigger difference.

WHY BUSINESS LIST SELECTION IS AN ART

Many mailers spend too little time on the development of mailing lists used to reach business prospects. Some say it is simple. If you are selling computers, all you've got to do is find a list of data processing managers. Right? Wrong! What you are really looking for is likely prospects who could benefit from a computer like yours. It may or may not be the data processing manager. There may not even be such a title in a prospective organization. It could be (1) the president in a smaller company, (2) the administrative vice president, (3) vice president, data processing, (4) director of MIS, (5) treasurer, (6) controller, (7) operations manager, (8) general purchasing agent, or many more titles.

That is just the beginning. There are many subclassifications, such as titles, types of industries, size, and so on, that can all have an effect on successfully targeting your promotion to best prospects.

The best way to broaden your horizon is by thinking about the true adage: "It is not what you have to sell, it is what the customer wants to buy." However, few marketers have the luxury of knowing just who wants to buy—and when.

To get a good start, there are some basic procedures that business mailers should use to find the best prospects.

Make a List of Product Uses

The right way to proceed is to make a list of all the possible uses of your product or service. Then, after each, list all of the job functions that could use or influence the use of your particular product or service.

We'll let you in on a secret. Don't make out the list yourself. Get help from others who designed, developed, marketed, and have sold the item. From experience and dreams, perhaps for years, they have been thinking about uses you may never have thought of.

As a next step, list the basic Standard Industrial Classification (SIC) categories that could use your item, based on your research above. A business list catalog will give you those categories— thousands of them.

Using a business list that has selectability on zip codes, industry classification, size, and so on, start building your list of prospects you wish to reach.

Guides to Better List Selection

There are many rules we've developed over the years that continue to be successful aids. Here are a few:

1. *Assume your salespeople's list is not good.* Probably the biggest mistake most marketers make is the assumption that their sales or representative's list of prospects is the only list you need. Unfortunately, salespeople only know who they know. They don't know who they don't know. Prove it to yourself. Take any Yellow Pages directory and see how many prospects are not on your house list. How can you expect your salesperson or representative to call, with sufficient frequency and breadth, on companies and on the *right* individuals? To earn their commissions, they go where they know the action is!

Business dynamics are such that businesses themselves often don't know when they will be in the market for a particular product or service. Play the odds by covering the logical candidates.

2. *Broaden your thinking.* While a prospect in-person call costs about $300 to make, a direct mail call costs about $1. Would you rather spend $300 on one person-to-person cold call or make 300 calls by mail? With these kinds of odds, you can afford to mail to more markets. You will be surprised with the results.

3. *Test your entire spectrum.* In performing the analysis we described above, you undoubtedly uncovered new areas. Mail at least a few hundred or, hopefully, a few thousand pieces to each. It takes that many pieces to get a feel. If you don't test the spectrum, you may be missing your best leads.

4. *Don't rely on salespeople's evaluation of a prospect (except on credit).*   We are always surprised how many good leads we get from places we mailed where we've been told there is no business.

5. *When in doubt, title address by function.*   Sometimes it is impossible to know the proper titles. Consider using "To the person in charge of lubricants," or "manager—lubricants," or "lubricant supervisor." When you don't know the proper formal title, you are, perhaps, more effective just being direct.

6. *Code each subselection.*   All labels have space for code lines. We suggest that you order SIC codes (four or five characters), title addressing code one digit. That still leaves room for mailing package codes and drop date and offer codes, if necessary. Most important of all, make sure you order counts for each subselection universe. Unless you know how many you mailed, you can't determine response rates. You have to design your piece so the label comes back.

7. *Use secondary classification.*   When you review a list of SIC codes, you will find secondary applications. That means that the classification is not the primary business of that firm. If it is a secondary business, they still need the products and services you offer.

Business list selectivity is a unique art unto its own. However, it is highly measurable. Data and leads you generate can make your sales manager think you are the greatest. Don't miss the opportunity.

WHY PSYCHOGRAPHICS ARE IMPORTANT

Direct mail did not become efficient and telemarketing did not really grow until segmentation entered the field of direct marketing.

The first big push was the zip code. Direct marketers moaned that the zip code would ruin the industry because no one would remember their zip code, and the cost for mailers would be prohibitive.

The reverse was true because it enabled segmentation to the mass market to take hold. Now direct marketers cannot afford *not* to zip code. Overlaid on zip codes was census data, enabling even further market segmentation. Then came the biggest boom, the great proliferation of mailing lists on the market, enabling further segmentation.

This great improvement of efficiency through list targeting was, unfortunately, offset by increases in postage, paper, and printing costs.

Additional segmentation is necessary if future expenses are to be offset so direct marketing can continue its growth. One of these avenues is psychographics. My definition of psychographics is simply subjective characteristics that affect buying habits. I divide psychographics into two parts. One is the study of how a person perceives advertising messages. The other is the particular life style, environment and/or personality traits that shape our likes and dislikes.

Psychographics and the Advertising Message

There is a powerful segmentation that only direct marketers can take advantage of—the right-brained person versus the left-brained person.

Everyone knows that the right brain controls left side movements and the left brain controls right side movements. The left brain also controls sequential activities: speech, mathematics, spelling, and reading.

While controversy rages, there is a considerable amount of evidence that indicates people are either left- or right-brain dominant. This could be reflected in being naturally left-handed or right-handed. Because the right brain is holistic rather than sequential, activities such as sports, painting, or design are right-brained activities. This is a partial explanation of why so many baseball players are left-handed. Based upon the aforementioned, it could be concluded that people who are right-brained respond to more holistic advertising messages such as pictures, logos, trademarks, and so on, whereas sequential people respond better to long copy.

The interesting fact is that direct marketers can compile a list of left-handers versus right-handers, which is the give-away symptom of left- or right-brain dominant individuals. This compilation is possible because in reading a given coupon, order form, or donation, left-handed writing can usually be detected.

The ability to reach the right- or left-brained person with the most appealing message form may be a big breakthrough in further segmentation. The industry has done well to isolate the previous mail order buyer—a most important and proven characteristic to higher direct marketing response.

Overall, however, creative segmentation has not followed list segmentation. In the future, mailers and telephone people will learn that it can be cost effective to write different copy to different audiences.

Psychographics and What You Buy

It is unreasonable to think that the ultimate computerization will be an analysis of your last 10 years' purchases to determine what you will buy during the next 10 years. But we have come farther than you might think.

Employees respond differently than owners because it is not their money. Owners want to save money because it goes into their pocket. Employees want less job hassle, and want to impress their supervisors in order to receive promotions and raises, and not risk losing their jobs.

Men react differently than women to color. Several years ago, I watched a panel of six men and six women react to a mail package. Not one of the men commented on its color. All the women commented on it. I learned many years ago to let women be the judges of color and design—especially if the target audience is female.

Upscale mailing has been one of the most exciting aspects of the recent mail order boom. Banks will learn which of their customers are into numbers and find an easier sell of television banking, telephone banking, and even automated teller machines.

Psychographics is a limitless area of specialization. It can't help but play an increasingly important role as targeting and specialization continue.

WHY MULTIMEDIA WORKS

The new buzz word in the early 1980s was multimedia direct marketing.

Test reports from all industries indicated that when you combine direct mail and telephone together, the combined effort is greater than each medium individually. In fact, the late Murray Roman, one of the true pioneers of telephone marketing, frequently said that when you combine telephone and direct mail, the results are three to five times the sum of each separately. Running 10 second spots, or longer, on television, telling people to look for the mail about to arrive in their mail box, seems to more than pay for itself.

Using both magazine ads offering catalogs and merchandise by mail and the cold list mailing of catalogs themselves seems to work, though the method is hard to qualify. The dramatic rise of mail order magazine ads testifies to the results. Remember, *everything* is measured in direct marketing.

Why this multimedia success? The answer lies in the fact that mass media is inexpensive, and the more direct the medium, the more expensive. On a relative index basis, with the cost of a page mass market magazine ad at $100, the following shows how expensive targeted mediums are on a cost per exposure basis:

Television spot	$ 50
Consumer magazine	$ 100
Trade magazine	$ 500
Direct mail	$ 5000
Telephone call	$60,000

Simply, if low cost media can favorably affect higher cost media, the leverage effect is enormous and the savings considerable.

Let's take an example. A mailing is made to announce to a doctor a new prescription drug product. The company offering it is not well known. The mailing talks about the benefit of the product, little-known facts about the company's fine history, and the excellent background of key executives.

Even if the doctor just glances at the piece, the doctor knows more about the company and product than before. Awareness is created.

The follow-up phone call to the doctor is more efficient for two reasons. First, the doctor, being aware, is more apt to accept the call. Second, less time need be spent establishing the company, because the doctor already has some awareness. This helps to reduce the total time of the phone call.

Phone calls, as we have seen, are very expensive. If you can reduce the time of the call by 20%, increase acceptance of a call by 20%, and receptivity by 20%, you have at least a 60% efficiency increase on a medium that is twelve times as expensive as direct mail.

You can relate multimedia efficiency in direct marketing to multimedia in general advertising. For example, an auto manufacturer will advertise its product in magazines, on television, on billboards, in newspapers, and so on. But it all comes down to bringing the prospect into the showroom and having the prospect presold, which saves the floor salesperson time and increases the chance of closing the sale.

Now that we know why, what does it tell us about how to plan a strategy for multimedia? It tells us to raise the lead media in such a way as to convey that part of the more expensive media story that can be explained the easiest and can reduce time the most.

A few test phone calls will quickly establish what hurdles your telemarketing effort faces. Some of these can be reduced or eliminated by a good softening campaign of direct mail.

Multimedia need not be expensive, just smart.

WHY SRDS IS A VERY IMPORTANT TOOL

I'm not here to sell SRDS books, but I refer to it more than all other direct marketing publications *combined.*

SRDS is short for Standard Rate and Data Service. If you are in advertising you know it well because there is one for every medium. The Newspaper SRDS gives all the rates and specifications for all newspapers. The Television SRDS does the same for television stations. Magazine SRDS, Radio SRDS, and Direct Mail Lists Rate and Data Services (DMLRDS) are other major publications.

The DMLRDS is a compendium of some 40,000 different mailing lists. It tells you more about different mailing lists than any other source because it encourages all list owners to include their lists, at no charge.

You can quickly find list areas (that is, gourmet, sports, education, and so on) and see what is available. Just being aware of what is available helps you talk to a list broker or manager (see section on list brokers). It helps you quickly find possible lists that you can refine with phone calls at a later date. But, more than that, the SRDS is a fund of marketing knowledge.

WHY LIST BROKERS MAY (OR MAY NOT) BE IMPORTANT

To the person new to direct marketing, the role of the list broker is confusing. Understanding what they do and why can help you utilize them more efficiently and know when not to use them.

First, there are many specializations within the list brokerage field, just as in real estate brokerage. Some specialize in consumer mail order, some in business. In direct marketing there are also list brokers who specialize in fund-raising.

The true list broker represents you, the person who wants to rent the best group of lists for your needs. The broker can have no tie to the list owner. If they did have ties to certain list owners, they could not be objective in selecting the right lists for you to use.

You, the list renter, are paying the bill. If a broker's recommendations work for you, you will be successful, be able to expand your business, and come back as a repeat customer. If a broker owned certain lists, or a percentage of those lists, and therefore pushed those lists in recommendations to you, you would have less chance of success, reducing any long-range business for the broker.

The list brokers have a huge advantage that will be more important to you than anything else. The better list brokers keep computer tabs on each list rental, including how many names have been rented and when they were rented. By reviewing this sheet and seeing a renter use the same list over and over, and taking larger and larger quantities of names available from that list, they know that list is working well for the product(s) or service(s). Multiply this information by the thousands of lists and thousands of list users and you have a very definitive fund of information.

Naturally, the broker can't tell you exactly who is doing what because it wouldn't be ethical. But the sum of this information is extremely valuable and will play an important part in the lists recommended to you.

Logic would say that the larger the broker, the more complete the data they have available. But, remember, "larger" must be defined in terms of the area of specialization that applies to your product or service. You can't go too far wrong in selecting a broker that also works for your bigger competitors.

The broker also handles all the paperwork of ordering, getting counts, and the follow-up for delivery that looks easy on the surface but becomes unbelievably complex. You will be surprised how much they do that you don't even think of. Unless you do random sampling and save names for continuation and counts, you must use a broker.

All we have said above also applies to the use of response lists. These are lists of mail order buyers, subscribers and inquiries. For compiled lists, you probably do not want to use a list broker.

Compiled lists are those such as household lists, auto registrations, drivers licenses, people listed in directories, businesses gleaned from Yellow Pages or credit reports, and so on. When you use compiled lists, you have much less choice of lists. They are usually larger in size (the whole county for household and telephone lists). The secret to success with compiled lists is selection. That means taking a factor or combination of factors that give you better results than a cross section of the list as a whole. Factors you can select include income, type of business, and literally hundreds more.

The reason you should go directly to the list owner on a compiled list is because the list owner knows more about that list than anyone else. They know which select factors work for various products or services offered. Compiled list owners have the knowledge of all the renters who rent direct and *all* the brokers who have used it on behalf of their clients.

As a rule of thumb, use a list broker when the choice of lists is wide; use a list owner when the choice is the segmentation within a list.

WHY YOU CANNOT AFFORD EXPENSIVE PROSPECTING

I get two or three a week and you probably get two or three a week: expensive, fancy mailings from people and places you've never heard of, obviously haven't done business with, and probably have no interest in doing business with. This is true of mail from merchandisers, services, fund-raising, as well as much business-to-business mail.

Then there is the other side. When you do raise your hand and show interest with a request for more information, what you receive, more often than not, is material that does not relate, and is not as exciting and interesting as the original piece that attracted your attention. Material comes late or does not come at all! By the time you receive it, you've lost interest. These mailers have got their promotional efforts backwards!

It makes sense to prospect with *low cost* mailings and follow up with more informative and exciting (thus more expensive) mailings, phone, or personal contact. In short, once you have a lead, let out all the stops to close the sale.

Here is why. When you are doing cold prospecting (that is, mailing to audiences where you don't know if they have any interest in your product or service), your chance of success is much lower than with someone who has already expressed interest. For example, your response from an interested party may be 10 or 20 times that of a cold list.

You would probably argue in rebuttal that unless you pull out all the stops and wave the flag the first time out, you'll never get the second chance. Wrong. This is where creativity comes in. With the right words and a few graphics, you can tease a person into responding, without telling or showing them too much. Later, hit them with a powerful mailing and/or information with a salesperson's arm attached.

Let's apply this concept to the various uses of mail.

1. *Business mail.* Few business sales are simple enough to close by mail, so this concept becomes very important. As Bob Hemmings, a leading expert on business mail for years, says, "tell the half-told tale." By the degree of information requested on the reply card, you can qualify your prospect. Later follow up with all your guns.

2. *Fund-raising.* When a prospect becomes a donor, they know and care about your project. Most fund-raising letters used

to find new contributors should be low cost. On this type of prospecting you don't personalize as much as you would with a former contributor because you haven't yet developed a relationship. It may be somewhat presumptuous if you do get too personal, and you might lose the prospect. But once a contributor, the more personalization the better.

3. *Consumer services.* Insurance, loans, clubs, and so on usually offer something simple for the first approach. Then they convert to more complex and expensive services once the prospect has become a customer. Expensive, complete mailings are sometimes affordable because the customer is a subscriber for years and years.

4. *Consumer merchandise.* We are referring to mail order catalogs here. To lower costs, a minicatalog is sometimes used in prospecting efforts, naturally featuring the most responsive items and special deals. Be careful here—it may be almost as cheap to mail the whole catalog. It depends on your printing economics. More and more minicatalogs are appearing because of this high cost of prospecting.

5. *Consumer books and magazines.* Our rule of prospecting at low cost and following up with a higher cost doesn't often apply here. Why? Two reasons seem important. One is direct mail's format, which permits as much discussion of a product as necessary to sell it at that time. The whole story can be told in one mailing. Magazines require graphics to get the true feel of the publication. If the close can't be made in one blockbuster mailing, it probably can't be made otherwise. There is nothing more to say that wasn't said the first time.

Remember, with most magazines the consumer is already familiar with the product. There is no more information to send. As a result, very few have found initial subscription phone follow-ups to be economical.

WHY DUPLICATION AND UNDELIVERABLE MAIL IS NOT A PROBLEM

We've just returned from a rather large meeting on direct mail. Much of the discussion concerned duplicate mailings to the same household.

Though experienced mailers don't worry about duplicate mail, fund-raisers do. They're probably more concerned because of public reaction. Volunteer members of boards of directors or auxiliaries of a fund-raising organization often receive more than one mailing. They erroneously feel the department responsible for mail is squandering hard-earned fund raising dollars.

Duplication Can Be Good

No, I'm not losing my marbles: duplication can be good. The best prospect for a donation is someone who gives to another cause. Even better are people who give to a few causes. The *very best* prospect is a person who gives to many other causes. Smart direct mail professionals have learned this and mail to as many of these people as possible. It stands to reason that the best prospect is the one who receives the most mail requesting funds.

When mailers use many lists to find new donors, they merge and purge the entries as a computer removes the duplications. Unfortunately, these purges are not perfect. A name may be misspelled on one list, zip code digits transposed on another. Unless the two duplicates are *exactly* the same, the computer probably will leave them both in. Thus, more duplicates appear in lists of heavy donors than in others.

Look at the results of two lists we tested.

List A. Response rate—3%; average gift—$10; duplication—15%.

List B. Response rate—2%; average gift—$10; duplication—3%.

For every thousand pieces mailed, $300 (30 × 10) was raised from List A, and only $200 from List B. Yet, duplication within List A was five times higher than in List B. In this case, duplication didn't count.

You Can Use Your Duplication Profitably

It was a surprise when the industry fund-raising pioneers found out that a second mailing, consisting of the culled duplicates, proved more profitable than going to other outside (or "cold") lists for unduplicated names.

Why? A duplicate has given to at least two causes, and is usually a much better prospect than a person who might have never given to anything at all.

Many mailers are mailing their duplicates in a second batch a few days (or as far as the list lender will allow) apart from the first mailing. Since they've already paid for the rental of these names, they might as well use them again.

This whole scenario can apply to commercial mail too. Some mailers send items to their customers up to 40 times a year! Consecutive mailings arrive on different days. Buying moods may vary.

There is no reason you can't change your offer (or theme) to these "duplicates" that are mailed twice. Simply a catalog cover or envelope change may be sufficient.

The Logic Behind It All

Some people don't give, react, or buy by mail at all. They claim they *never* buy by mail. They are lousy prospects that are almost guaranteed not to open your mailing piece. So why bother? They are a lost cause. The only way not to mail to them is to limit your mailing to customers of someone who sells, seeks, or informs by mail. That is where the action is. This means that the more duplicates you find among other people's customer list of mail order buyers or donors, the stronger the mail order characteristics. And, the stronger the characteristic, the better chance for a response.

Caution: The Optimum Is Not Mailing All Duplicates

Taking this rationale to the ultimate degree, mailers would seek only duplicates. Not so. Not only is such a list almost impossible to put together, but if you mailed only duplicates, you would reduce the number of new donors or customers. There are just enough of those heavy buyers or givers out there.

Direct mail is like most everything else. Do it in moderation. But don't throw out good lists just because somebody complained about duplication. Duplication is usually a good sign.

WHY YOU CAN USE SOMEBODY ELSE'S CUSTOMER LIST

Billions of names are mailed each year that are someone else's customers. Somebody else's customers will work better for you than directory lists. Why do people let others, even competitors, use their names? The primary reason is money. Rental income is sizeable and there are few costs applied against it. It is the kind of money that goes right to the bottom line.

To start with, people are not upset that you are renting your mailing list because they probably don't know it is being rented. People don't know whose list is whose, nor do they think in terms of renting a mailing list. They respond because they want what is offered, and you've given them good service in the past.

Renting your customer names for a profit to a *noncompetitor* doesn't hurt your business in any way. People don't budget how much they spend on direct mail or mail order, they budget how much they spend overall—including retail, door-to-door, or home party.

If you rent to a noncompetitor, some of your customers will respond to the noncompetitor's offer. But they will never know they were *your* customer when they did so. People can't really tell from labels what list they are on and don't pay any attention. So, by renting your names, you have received income you wouldn't have otherwise received. And it is very profitable income.

Now, let's talk about renting to or from competitors. The least invasive way is to rent "inquiries." These are people who identified themselves as being very interested in your products or services, but have not bought. Why not risk it? You could convert them to a sale. Your competitor will say they couldn't—so some income, name rental income, is better than no income!

How about renting your good customers to competitors? There is a way to do that so both sides are happy. Trade. I'll give you 10,000 of my good customers if you will give me 10,000 of your good customers. Billions of names are traded each year this way. The surprise is that *both* sides do better. Both sides make money. This works because no two people have exactly the same product, at the same price, of the same quality, tied to the same offer, communicated the same way, or mailed at the same time.

The mailed-at-the-same-time aspect needs explanation because it is, perhaps, the most important factor. You can't be everything to everybody and mail to everyone every week or you end up going broke. You can't mail, phone or advertise often enough to reach everyone at that perfect moment when they feel the need is strong enough to act, and they have the money to do so. Let someone else rent your lists when you are not mailing. However, don't let them mail your list just before you mail.

If I'm mailing a catalog out every three months, I can't afford to mail out every month. But if someone else's catalog, mailed four times a year, hits between my catalog drops, they will certainly capture a segment of the market that is ready and willing to buy.

In the gift area holiday merchandise, problems do arise at certain times of the year for gift items and fund-raisers. The pre-Christmas period is such a time. Wise list owners specify the time that renters can mail. This is certainly an important factor in fund-raising. You don't want your offer to be received the day after the receipt of two other solicitations.

Don't be afraid to get the most out of your lists by renting or trading.

LARGE VERSUS SMALL SPACE MAIL ORDER ADS

As we have discussed elsewhere, space advertising in newspapers and magazines is used either as a prospecting device, or to actually sell merchandise, or both.

The most common example of the ads used to prospect are the small space—1/6 or 1/12 of a page—black and white ads, that appear in the back of many consumer magazines, such as *House & Garden, Cosmopolitan, Popular Mechanics* or *Bon Appetit.* These ads sell merchandise, as well as offer their various catalogs.

The other extreme represents examples of full-page or large space ads, which are the traditional ads that sell a fairly complex mail order service, product, or line of products. By their very nature, they tell a complex story and are often "one-shots," meaning they are the only product in the line.

When to use large space and when to use small space is fairly clearly defined. The role of mail order sales versus lead generation cannot be reversed. That is, you cannot profitably use large space prospecting for a catalog or small space to really sell a complex product.

Let's consider a catalog marketer selling Early American furniture. The company offers hundreds of items in their catalog and uses space advertising, in small space, in selected magazines to get leads. They then send their full catalog to these leads.

This firm uses small space ads because the nature of their product is almost self-explanatory. Or it is at least self-explanatory enough to get a request for a catalog. Everyone who is interested in Early American furniture knows the style of a bed, chair, lamp, wall hanging, and so on, so they send for the catalog to find out the specifics.

One of the biggest mistakes catalog marketers with a few stores make is to assume that their stores and catalog name is known well enough nationally to allow them to just offer their catalog by name, maybe providing too brief of a description.

It took Neiman Marcus years and years to develop a national name, so they can just offer the Neiman Marcus catalog and everyone will know just what it is.

This failure to entice readers with contents becomes especially evident in those "catalog sections" that show scores of catalogs and offer a handy card to reply by circling the one or ones you want.

Since most catalog marketers charge a modest price for their catalog, in order to qualify these inquiries (a person who pays cold cash for a catalog should be a more serious buyer than one who sends for something free), a further description of the catalog's contents becomes more important. Sometimes it takes more effort to sell a catalog, whose contents are unknown, for a modest sum than it does to sell an accurately described product.

Small space ads must be brief. A 1/6-page ad costs about 1/6 as much as a full-page ad, or slightly more. Yet, both the large ad and the small ad have certain mandatory copy, such as where to send, price, product name, and company name. Let's say this takes up one-third of a small space ad. It could take up only 1/18 of a large space ad. One would falsely conclude the large space ad is more efficient. Wrong. Being six times larger doesn't mean you will get six times the response, because the person really interested in Early American furniture will probably be stopped by both ads. You don't need six times the space to get a lead from someone you've already stopped.

Small space ads can get away with more shortcuts too. They don't always need a coupon. Just say "Send to . . . " They can use short phrases, like those you see in classified ads.

The proof of the pudding is to look through a magazine and see how many large size ads you see that offer a catalog with one or two standard merchandise items. Notice I said standard merchandise items. You will note that small space ads always show something that has rather unusual appeal (to appeal to the broadest market) and that it is instantly understood as to what it is.

That brings us to the justification of the large space ads. If you think back to what large space mail order ads you have seen recently, they will have been for things like weight reduction, a new concept in a product or service, an insurance offer, a beauty product, or maybe a book.

These are items that are new, or are, if you'll pardon the pun, a new wrinkle on an existing product. That means a complex explanation is in order and, since these are pretty complex fields, some hard sell is necessary. People must be persuaded that they need the product or service, that this one is truly different, and that we are the right people to bring it to you with guaranteed quality and at a fair price.

The large ads must first stop you, which is not easy. The reader is probably not looking for the product because, being a new concept, they have never heard of it. That is why these ads often use a famous personality as an endorsement. The recognition of the famous personality stops the reader. Because the story is complex and because people are basically lazy and don't like to read, it is absolutely necessary that the flow be proper in a large size ad. That means: needs to benefits to features to guarantee to call to immediate action. As you become more proficient, you can slowly reduce the size of large ads. Testing to find out what the major points are that get the response will guide you.

In small space ads, if you find you are having a big success, you can go slightly larger and have the advertising pay for itself.

A reminder to let the media do the work for you is important. If you're selling Early American furniture in a magazine that is almost all about Early American furniture, you know your audience is keenly aware of your product line, so you need less space for explanation. If you are selling jogging clothes, you are helped by the fact that you are advertising in a jogging magazine.

Where the problem comes in is in those situations where you are in a broad based magazine and your product or service doesn't naturally fit. In these cases, it is usually worth the extra money for the large size ad to properly explain your product or service.

By appearing in the mail order section of a magazine, you are saying that you are a mail order product or service. Therefore, you do not need the dramatic coupon to remind the mail order reader to stop and read your ad.

SEVEN

LEAD GENERATION AND DEALER SUPPORT

WHY THE SALES MANAGER'S ROLE IS CHANGING

We've always thought of the sales manager as the person with the glib tongue, the well-pressed suit, the ability to charm anyone into a sale, or the man with the whip for the sales force.

Tomorrow's sales manager is going to be different. Why? There are two reasons. The first is that the average sales call is approaching $300 in cost. The second is that basically people don't like to sell. Tomorrow's sales manager may well be a direct mail specialist!

Fortunately, a well directed direct mail program resolves both of these reasons. A few companies are effectively utilizing the medium, yet most have not even scratched the surface of its potential.

Let's talk first about preselling, or lead generation. A major responsibility of a sales manager is to devise a system where prospects will identify themselves. Obviously, the way to get somebody to identify themselves is to have them ask you for more information about what you have to sell. There are no better vehicles to do this than through direct mail or couponed space advertising in select business publications. In the latter, I suspect that image advertising will be on the way out and lead generating advertising on the way in.

There are many ways to get people to identify themselves. These include the use of premiums, exciting copy, promises; and benefits. Prospects will identify themselves, providing you make it easy for them. That means just having to check a box and drop the already filled out business reply card in the mail.

More Follow-Ups

The second assignment of a sales manager will be more frequent follow-ups. Although most salespeople won't admit it, much of their success is due to being at the right place at the right time. In other words, to be on the spot at the time the prospect becomes interested. Through direct mail and increased trade magazine advertising, you can be on the spot more often and at the right time. It never ceases to amaze us when following up the leads to our own advertising, to find that the prospect has responded because our mailing came at the right time. Timing is paramount. Mailing is cheap, advertising is cheap—far cheaper than a sales call. Frequency of advertising will play an increasingly more important role.

Different companies have different needs or requirements as to the quality of leads they need. Some just want a warm body. Once the salesperson gets in the door they know they can achieve a high close rate. Others need highly qualified leads because the sales call is too expensive unless the prospect has a good chance of being converted to a customer. Great strides have been made in the direct marketing business to control the flow and quality of leads to the sales force. Here, more than anywhere else, the sales manager becomes a true direct mail specialist to provide just the right amount of leads to each salesperson.

Now there's a second area where the sales manager should become a direct mail specialist—the area of reorders. While we've already shown how expensive it is to make a sales call on a prospect, it is also becoming increasingly more expensive to make a sales call to sell additional products or services to many of your present customers. Here's where telephone selling, space coupon ads, and direct mail order forms come to the forefront. The largest office supply companies are learning this lesson well, and are utilizing the telephone to call on their smaller customers, giving their salesmen more time to call on the bigger customers. Techniques are being developed so the smaller customers identify themselves when they have the need for a major item that is worth a salesperson's visit. For example, you can sell duplicating machine fluid by mail or telephone very easily. But you want the customers to identify themselves when they need a new machine.

Three Accomplishments

Yes, tomorrow the sales manager will say, "I'm cutting my sales force by 25%, putting that money into a target direct mail and trade magazine prospecting program, coupled with a direct mail follow-up program to my present customers. I'll accomplish several things at the same time. First, I'll get more customers because I reach people my sales force could never have time to reach. Second, I'll get more business from my present customers because I will reach them more often and when they are ready to buy. Third, my customers will be happier because they'll be spending less time listening to a salesperson's pitch because they will call us only when they are ready to buy." There's something in it for everybody.

WHY DIRECT MAIL INCREASES SALES FORCE EFFICIENCY

Increase Sales Force Efficiency by 50 Percent—Free

Now, there is a headline that should get your attention. So, right up front I'll tell you how, and then spend the rest of this chapter proving it to all the doubting Thomases. It's simple. Cut your sales force in half. Then develop a sophisticated direct mail program on a continuing basis with the budget formerly earmarked for your terminated sales force. Or, said another way, transfer the expense of the weakest half of your sales force to a direct mail program.

To understand the logic of this radical proposal, we must first look at a typical sales force. The old law comes into play. The best 30% generate over 70% of the business. And you already know which is the 30%. Direct mail by itself becomes a unique kind of sales force. Here is why. The biggest mistake firms make is to only mail to their customer or salesperson's prospect list.

Salespeople Don't Know Who They Don't Know . . .

More explicitly, "salespeople know who they know, but don't know who they don't know." You'd be amazed how big this "don't know" area is in your own sales organization. It has to be because no salesperson can cover all these bases:

- A new person assigned to your area of opportunity in a company you may have been calling on.
- A company branches out into a new area that could suddenly need your product or service.
- Other departments in a firm you are calling on could use your product or service.
- New technology makes your product fit.

Not long ago, we obtained a direct mail account because the chairman of the board of a Fortune 500 company, a billion-plus dollar operation, asked why his marketing people were not using direct mail. Frankly, we would never have thought in a million years to call on him!

There are others like him. Where we could never get in, our direct mail might. There is nothing more influential in a company than a note from the highest authority saying, "You might want to look into this."

Direct Mail Reaches Hidden or Latent Opportunities

The biggest mistake firms mailing to other businesses make is to only mail to their customer or salesperson's prospect list.

Fortunately, once an area for prospecting has been selected, there are business lists that can reach close to 100% of that profile.

What is your profile, you ask? It is easy to come by. Profile your present customers. There are always many more out there with similar profiles who could be prospects too. Common profile factors you can match with direct mail lists include SIC code (industry classification), geographic, business sales size, number of employees, branch versus headquarters, and so on.

Most business mailings are relatively small. Therefore, most of the cost is in the developing of the mailing. Printing and mailing a few more has little increase in cost on an incremental basis.

The Second Biggest Mistake

After failure to mail to a broad enough list of companies, the next most common mistake is not mailing to enough people *within* a company. This problem divides itself into several parts.

1. *Prospects.* This, obviously, is the basic group. These are the people who most often raise their hands and express interest, or are known to buy your product or service. They want to do their job better and your product or service may help.

2. *Decision influencers.* Very few influencers will help you. Most will hinder you because they find it easier to say no to expenditures. The person who often asserts the most negative influence is the financial officer. Financial people get paid to say "no." Direct mail offers a unique opportunity to reach those people and tell your story the way you want it told, and eliminate the negatives in their minds.

3. *R&D/planners.* This group can be the most productive of the lot. They are at the headwaters of new developments. Chief of research, chief of engineering, long-range planners, and quality controllers are all people who could find new uses for your product. Perhaps they will find ones you or your organization never thought of because your organization had no way of knowing all of the developments in other fields. New developments are usually more secretive, and your sales organization

would have less chance to learn of the opportunity. Companies' problems are often kept secret, so your company has no chance to offer a remedy. Use direct mail to all these titles. The spark or generation of an idea your mail gives off could lead them to just the answer they are looking for.

Third Biggest Mistake

The third biggest mistake is not mailing often enough. You just never know when someone will have an interest in something you have to sell. Out of sight, out of mind! If they don't remember you, you'll never get a call. In insurance, it is called "X" date— the date a present policy expires. It's tough to sell when someone has just renewed his policy, but, at the right time, it could be easy.

Mail Does Not Have to Be Expensive

Most good direct mail, especially in the business-to-business field, is usually not fancy, thus, not expensive. Good mail usually has two strong features. First, it is directed to the right audience. Second, it is straightforward and to the point. Now it is up to a salesperson to take over.

That's where we started. The direct mail half of your sales force has generated a lead. You've gotten the good half of your sales force intact. They are the tigers. They are the ones working around the clock, and who can do the best job of selling.

Since leads will convert to sales perhaps 10 times more effectively than cold calls, the result is more sales per effort. Perhaps a 50% increase!

WHAT REALLY HELPS DEALERS MOST

Much business mail is dealer related. However, few advertisers are willing to look at the dealer's point of view before they start developing their advertising programs. Direct mail can work wonders if you look at it through the eyes of the dealer. Start with the assumption that the individuals at the dealer level, whether they be retail clerks, local salespeople, or the dealers themselves, care nothing about what you have to sell. They have lots of different things to sell other than your product or service.

You have heard us say before, "It is not what you have to sell, but what the customer wants to buy." Your dealer's feelings fit right into this concept. From the time they are weaned, they are concerned with what their customers want to buy. So you had better look from their side of the counter.

Next, assume a dealer or his staff is going to do nothing to help you. Why should they? How are you any different than any other vendor or supplier they represent? "What's in it for me?" No matter how good your deal, I'll bet someone has a better deal.

Now we've cleaned the slate. How do we get off square one? Direct mail, in many cases, is a good place to start—if done correctly.

Use Direct Mail to Profile Your Market

Find the universe of people who might buy and those who do buy. Send out a questionnaire. We've developed a system to get 30% to 50% response. You can too. Then analyze your results. Look for two things: profile of those who bought, and profile of those who didn't buy. Then compare the two. How are they different? Now you have a concept of who you are trying to reach with your advertising. If no one else, your copywriter and media people will thank you. (By the way, do the design and analysis of your research yourself. Don't expect a tabulator to find the skews, as most may be semihidden. It takes someone with a great deal of knowledge about the business to sense and interpret the subtleties.)

Use Direct Mail to Precondition Your Dealers and Salespeople

This works two ways. Most people with sales titles really don't like to sell—especially cold call selling. A direct mailing to their prospects can perform miracles. The fact that a mailing is going out forces the sales and dealer people to take a moment to understand your product and promotion—they realize they will be asked, because of the mailing, and they don't want to appear stupid. You've at least got their attention.

Something else equally important will happen. Because the mailing was made, the salespeople will consciously or subconsciously feel that the person they must contact is *expecting* to be contacted. In their mind, it is no longer a cold call, but rather a friend. You have already built up a line of communication between seller and prospect. The salesperson looks forward to making the call, rather than dreading it. There is another related benefit. The mailing does part of the selling job, thus reducing the time the salesperson must spend trying to make the sale.

In telephone marketing, it is absolutely essential that mail precede a phone call to precondition the recipient so that less phone time is required—as phone time is *very* expensive.

Use Direct Mail to Find Prospects

If you are trying to find new customers, the *worst* list you can use is a salesperson's list. The salesperson doesn't know about prospects that haven't surfaced. There are always a lot of people out there who are new—new companies or firms who were never thought to be prospects but are now prospects because of changing needs, new people at prospect companies, and people who have changed job responsibility within a firm. It is almost impossible for anyone to keep up, especially a dealer or salesperson. What you want to do is reach the people your salespeople don't even know about.

Mail from Headquarters—Not a Dealer or Branch

We have found that the fine support effort a dealer is providing on your behalf is the biggest misconception clients have. It should be an axiom that much *less* materials supplied to dealers will be used by these dealers than even your most conservative estimate. It is even gloomier when you realize how poor a dealer's mailing list probably is for the pieces that dealers are using.

Time after time, clients tell us about their great program of supplying stuffers to use in dealer invoices to other businesses. Of course, they haven't coded the stuffers, so they don't really know what is happening. But an invoice stuffer is the *worst* possible way to advertise to a business. You see, the invoice goes to the accounting department. This department's prime function is to lower expense. They don't believe in spending money for anything. Thus, they have more reason to throw your stuffer in the wastebasket than anyone else in the company!

By doing your mailing from central headquarters to the markets you've profiled, your chance of success is much greater. It will get to the best prospects. The salespeople will find them to be good leads and improve their close ratio.

Use Direct Mail for Follow-Up

The person contacted may not buy today but may buy tomorrow. Keep in contact with a series of mailings that bring up additional points of why to buy. Add others above and around your contact to your mailing list. You never know who is the real decision maker, or who will be in your prospect's job tomorrow.

Direct mail does a great deal more than what it is given credit for. The sales department will say that the resulting success was all because of their great selling ability and not promotion. What do you care . . . you've got the added business!

EIGHT

TELEPHONE

WHY TELEPHONE DIRECT MARKETING IS SO SUCCESSFUL—OUTBOUND

Since about 1980, the rise of telephone marketing, or telemarketing, has been nothing short of phenomenal. Why is telephone suddenly working so well and finding its own? Because marketing professionals are learning how to use telephone.

Telephone calls are expensive. Labor is on a one-to-one basis, it is difficult to get through, and the cost of a call is expensive. Telephone runs somewhere between the cost of direct mail and the cost of a sales call. Because it is so expensive, users have had to harness this power efficiently by (1) reducing the time of a call, (2) providing lists with a greater potential for positive response, and (3) learning closing techniques.

Reducing the time of a call is best understood if one realizes that all costs are direct, and neither labor nor phone call costs are reduced as volume increases. Therefore, it becomes very important to reduce the length of the call.

This is best done by preinforming the prospect, using a low cost medium. For example, if a direct mail piece describes what the offer is, why it is good for you, the features, and who the organization is that is making the offer, then that does not have to be repeated when the call is made.

Further, with advance knowledge of what the call is all about, the recipient has time to consciously or subconsciously think about it. Increased knowledge should give the seller a better chance to close a sale.

It is safe to say that the softening up of direct mail not only reduces the time required of the phone follow-up but also provides insights that increase the chances of a close.

More accurate mailing lists are of prime importance to the success of a phone program. The chance of random phone book look-ups being successful is slim. The chance of present or past customers responding is far greater.

The more targeted the list, the better the chance phone will work. That is why phone solicitation works well for: raising funds from past contributors, members of an association responding to an association or association-supported offer, inquiries, people clearly defined, past users, friends of past users, and so on.

In direct mail, a list of people who have responded to *any* direct mail offer are better than those who have not. Similarly, those who respond once to a telephone offer have a greater chance of responding to another telephone offer, even though there is no relation between product or service.

Closing techniques have become a real art. Most calling programs are mass market programs. That means hundreds or thousands of calls. When numbers become large, one must modularize the system so that all phone operations are using the same system and techniques—those which have *proved* to be the best.

Fortunately, it is easy to improve the technique. By simply

trying a new innovation, offer, or way of expressing something, one can determine if it works.

One of the great advantages of phone selling is the feedback one hears. Over a period of days, if the same problem or barrier exists, it can be studied and new techniques to remove the barrier can be used.

There are other reasons for telephone's success. One is the greater acceptance of phone solicitation. The younger generation has learned that the phone is a real time-saver. People who use the phone more themselves are often better prospects for phone selling.

Improved hardware, use of taped testimonial interviews, and the greater sophistication of the telephone solicitors help too.

WHY TELEPHONE DIRECT MARKETING IS SO SUCCESSFUL—INBOUND

Inbound is receiving calls generated by the customer or prospect but paid for by you. The 800 number system is the best example.

The people who can best measure are direct marketers who receive data on every order. There are two schools of thought on whether the use of an 800 number is really cost efficient.

On the plus side for the 800 number is the fact that it is *free* to the purchaser. This may encourage a telephone order that would otherwise be a mail order or no order at all.

People with products that require a great deal of information, because it can be purchased a myriad of ways, find that telephone ordering generates orders they may not otherwise have obtained. It does this in two ways. It keeps the response simple. That includes all the complexities of questions that must be asked, or hidden from the responders until they are face-to-face, or phone-to-phone, with an experienced communicator. This expert can put a sale back on the track if he or she perceives the prospect may be backing off. Second, phone follow-up assures the complex order has been placed correctly and is fully acceptable to both sides.

People who use 800 number selling usually have a program to sell something else to the customer at the time they place their order. "We have white widgets on sale this week at 50% off to our valued telephone customers. How many widgets would you like?" Or "We are out of stock of the blue you requested. I'm sure the new beige we have in would be just right." This enables a direct marketer to substitute overstocked merchandise for back-ordered merchandise.

By far the biggest aid to inbound telephone ordering is the rise of the bank debit cards. Owning a MasterCard or Visa Card makes the ordering very easy, and allows you to spend more than what you thought you could spend because of the debit card's credit line.

On the negative side of 800 number inbound calls is the cost of phone time. On how many of these calls would you have received these orders anyway?

The industry is about 50/50 on whether to offer 800 numbers or require the prospect or customer to pay for these calls. But, when you break it down by categories, this 50/50 changes. Department stores are big users. Those people who sell the type of merchandise that invites a lot of questions tend to stay away from 800 numbers. This includes cookware, as people want to talk about recipes and why something did or did not turn out. The same is true for home repairs ("How do you fix it?") and, perhaps, color related items ("Do you think pink or blue would look best?"). When used correctly, 800 numbers are hard to beat.

NINE

CREATIVE

WHY CONSUMER MAIL AND BUSINESS MAIL ARE SO DIFFERENT

Before we get too far into the creative or visual aspect of a mailing package, a careful look into the difference in strategies between mail going to a business and mail directed to a residence is important.

THE PRICE OF THE PRODUCT OR SERVICE

Whether the selling price of the product or service you are offering is high ticket (hundreds or thousands of dollars) or low ticket (5, 10, 20, or 50 dollars) determines the nature of the mailing or phone effort.

If the ticket is high enough to warrant a salesperson replying in person or by phone, then the object is to get a lead. The salesperson will explain and close in person or by phone. If the ticket is too small for a salesperson's time, then the sale must be concluded by the mailing. That means telling and describing everything.

Most consumer mail is low ticket. Most business mail is high ticket. Therefore, most business mail is to generate leads.

The two exceptions to this are seminars and office products. Seminars are usually higher ticket, but they operate on low margins and usually can't afford a sales force. The mailing must do the job. Office products catalogs have replaced salespeople on all but the biggest accounts. Thus, office products catalogs close the sale, just as a consumer catalog does.

THE PROBLEM OF MULTIPLE DECISION-MAKING

In business, there may be from 2 to 10 decision-makers. This means a sale cannot be conducted with one mailing to one person. Your story must be received by several. Often, the personal sales intervention solves that. Also, these different decision-makers must be spoken to in different ways.

In the home there is one, or at the most, two, decision-makers. Fortunately, they can usually be spoken to in the same way.

The Problem of Complexity

High ticket items are most often more complex than low ticket items. There are usually many more options to select.

In low ticket items to the consumer, the important thing to remember is: *Keep it simple!* The more choices consumers must make, the more confused they will become, and the result may be that they back off and do nothing.

Formality versus Personalization

You rarely see margin notes in business mail. You rarely see stilted prose in writing to a consumer. Right or wrong, business mail is more formal. Frankly, too formal. But, if you get informal, you may lose. The great copywriters succeed because they can blend a warmth into a business communication without being too obvious.

The Offer

The offers are different between business and consumer. Unless the business is a very small one, the person receiving the mail is dealing with someone else's money. It is not theirs. A money-saving offer does not work as well in these cases. An offer to your home is talking directly to *your* wallet!

Time

Many direct marketers profess that business people have less time than people at home. Frankly, many households are busier than many people at business. In an age where both spouses work, time is at a premium more than ever before. Time doesn't appear to be the main factor in why brief mailing efforts work better to business. The time available for the amount of mail (including interoffice memos) received at business versus home is a valid reason. But if the initial tease or offer is appealing, it will work at either home or office.

Remember these principles as we get more specific about parts of a mailing package.

THE IMPORTANCE OF ENVELOPES

Generally speaking, a direct mail effort in an envelope will out-pull a self-mailer (that is, a double or multiple fold post card).

Envelopes work. First, they set the stage. Like it or not, the person you are mailing to is more apt to react to a direct mail effort that comes in an envelope. There is something about self-mailers that appears more as "junk mail" and, therefore, less important.

In business, executives and managers sometimes say they don't want to see junk mail—and they define junk mail as these loud, fold-over postcards. The envelope sets the stage for a personal letter, and personal letters must be read.

The next thing envelopes do is to provide a vehicle to tease the reader into reading the mailing package. The tease can be expressed many ways.

1. *Teaser headline.*   My favorite teaser is "Your Salary Survey Enclosed." A good teaser forces you, out of curiosity, to open the letter.

2. *Envelope question.*   Ask a question and you may find yourself in trouble. "Do You Need White Hosiery?" Maybe I don't. If so, the letter would go right into the wastebasket—unopened.

If the headline asks: "Do You Want To Save Money On Hosiery?," you are in much better shape. Every woman thinks she wants to save money on hosiery.

Don't even ask a question the reader can say "no" to.

3. *No envelope copy.* Sometimes the best teaser of all is to say nothing. Here you are at the mercy of your firm's business. If the mailing comes from my bank, I've got to open it. If it is from Box 100, Boulder, Colorado, maybe I'll just toss it in the waste basket.

An envelope can be a picture frame. If you are including a beautiful color brochure within your mailing package, why not show it off through a clear, plastic envelope—or window envelope.

An envelope can be a graphic tease. Teasers don't have to be all copy. They can tease graphically, as a small window through which peeks a valuable coin, token or prize, or a pretty pink envelope, or paper stock of such quality that the reader must open it. Teasers can be graphically down scale too. A brown Kraft (shopping bag) paper can denote value.

The Reply Envelope

Why bother? If you expect money or a check by return mail, or if the information coming back may be perceived by the sender as confidential, you'd better enclose an envelope.

Our society is too lazy to look for an envelope. If you expect your reader to supply one, you will probably be in for a big surprise. When you make your offer more complicated by making your customer or prospect find and address an envelope, the chances are that they may never get around to it.

Reply envelopes don't need to be, and shouldn't be, fancy. They should give the feeling of straightforward importance—that they will deliver your reply correctly and promptly. If you do anything, add to this sense of urgency with copy like "Rush" or "Immediate Attention Required."

Long flap envelopes work and they are economical, which is why they are so popular. The industry calls them "bang tail" envelopes. Almost all department stores use them in their billing. They sell on the flap, and you return the flap.

Large versus Small Envelopes

There is no one answer here. To start off, the inside contents determine the size of envelopes. Arguments in favor of large envelopes include impact, look of importance, and a larger billboard to convey a more complex or more graphic message.

Arguments against large envelopes include added expense, the fact that some readers perceive them as more "junk mailish" than a regular #9 or #10 envelope, such as a personal letter is carried in, and they go to the bottom of the day's incoming mail, with smaller envelopes on top.

Both sizes work because they are used when it makes sense to use them.

Why Most Mail Has a Window for the Address

The overriding reason is that the mailing usually involves a test, with an identification code on the name and address label to identify the respondent—which mailing list they were on, what offer, and which mailing package they were sent. Results are tabulated carefully. The label comes back with the response card.

If there was no window, the coding would be on the envelope label and would never be returned.

As we have said before, good direct marketing is performing a thousand little details *correctly*. An envelope plays an important role. By itself, it will appear as nothing. Together, in a well integrated mailing package, it plays a harmonious part.

WHY LONG LETTERS?

When you have to make a sale by mail, the chances are that your direct mail letter is not long enough. Don't pay attention to anyone who says your letter is too long.

Why? When you are selling by mail to consumers, your one chance for a sale is the mailing package your readers have in their hands. No salesman will even call. There is no other chance to answer a reader's questions. There is no chance for a one-to-one, personal, hard close. This one mailing must do it all.

We know we are right. You can easily test in direct mail. Many have tested short letters versus long letters to consumers, and the long letter almost always wins. So, the industry knows what it is talking about through experience.

A letter must give every reason to buy that could possibly arise in a reader's mind, and answer every reason not to buy. You can't do all that on a one-page letter. You're a skillful writer if you can do it in four pages.

At least once a week I hear, "I never read long letters." Upon pursuing this statement, I find what the person meant to say was, "I never read long letters unless I am very interested in the subject." This has an important relationship to basic direct mail marketing principles. Let us say you mail to 100,000 prospects. For our case, assume that four percent purchase, which is 4000 customers. This is your hard core. Many would have bought the item no matter how it was presented, even if it was written by hand on brown wrapping paper. But what about the marginal buyers?

Converting to sales those-who-almost-bought is the "make or break" of direct mail. You don't care about the 90% who wouldn't buy if it was delivered on a gold platter. That is the group that "never reads long letters." Your effort is targeted to the 6% who are interested but not yet buyers. On a 100,000 mailing, in our example, that is 6000 good prospects. If it is a $20 sale and you convert half, that is an additional $60,000 in extra sales.

This "almost bought" group will read your letter, no matter how long—just as long as it remains interesting to them. Keep it interesting and you can write pages that they will read.

One of the most productive letters ever written was to fill up a plane to take an around-the-world tour of the North and South Poles. An eight page letter by Hank Burnett sold out the plane! It is a direct mail classic.

When you are mailing to businesses, chances are your letter is too long. Your goal is lead generation, to set an appointment for a salesperson. In business mail, deals are way too large and complex to sell by mail. You can't sell a custom-made steel furnace by mail. All you want to do is get your salesperson's foot in the door. If you tell it all, what does the prospect need a salesperson for? You must whet their appetite or tease them. One of the most successful mailings we ever did was a program that sold three times more computer software than the most optimistic projection. The letter was just three short paragraphs. It generated more leads than anyone expected. Then the salespeople really did a follow-up job.

Now, let's talk about business mail. At the onset of any discussion, common terminology must be established. There are two kinds of business mail.

1. *Mail order business mail.* This is a marketing effort that sells products or services directly to business organizations. The reader responds with an order directly to the advertiser, who ships

the order directly to the business. Popular examples are office supply catalogs, seminar offerings, and office equipment.

2. *Business-to-business lead generation.* Respondents are asked to identify themselves (accept an offer, send in for a premium, request more information, and so on). This response goes to a company's sales force, distributor, wholesaler, or dealer for follow-up. It is up to the salesperson to close the sale. It is lead generation.

The principles of *mail order* business mail, from a creative standpoint, do not vary significantly from consumer mail order principles. So, little will be discussed herein on mail order. Business-to-business lead generation mail, on the other hand, has vastly different principles and will be discussed in depth.

Basic Direct Mail Principles Unique to Business Mail

There are scores of direct mail principles that apply to all kinds of direct mail. They are just good mail principles, period. The purpose of this segment, however, is to dwell on *differences.* The key to understanding the differences between consumer and business mail principles is to understand the differences between the two audiences.

1. In business, readers may not be spending their own money. Other benefits, like promotion, recognition, and reduced work, may become more important.
2. Many more people are involved in business decisions. You can make your own decision at home, but how often do you make *buying* decisions at work?
3. In business, the true decision maker is usually hidden.

4. The item or service being offered to business is usually much higher priced than consumer items. Quite bluntly, businesses have more needs and more money to spend than individuals.

5. Because these business items are more complex and more expensive, salespeople, on a one-to-one basis, are essential to the close. Therefore, lead generation becomes very important in business mail.

6. Less is usually known about the mail order characteristics of the recipient in business mail. Much of business mail is title addressed, so mail order purchasing characteristics often do not exist.

7. In business, the impulse buy is less frequent. Companies have policies that any expenditure, no matter how small, must be approved by at least one other person. Business mail is just not as simple as calling up and giving your bank card number.

8. Business also has less time to read. Effective direct mail must not only stop the reader, but must also get the story to the busy, scanning reader. This may well be the most important of the differences from consumer mail.

How Business Mail Creative Packages Differ

Let's look at some of the most important and different aspects:

1. *Short letters to business.* Long letters are for mail order, but short letters prevail for business mail. Why? Because the object is to tease, bribe, or induce the reader to want to see a salesperson. It is up to the salesperson to close the sale. The salesperson can answer all the prospect's reasons not to buy, both in person and by phone. Lead generating letters should be less

than one page. The long letters for consumer mail are necessary to provide the answers for every reason the prospect can think of not to buy. The one letter is the only chance to close the sale with the consumer.

2. *Sell the offer, not the product.* The free offer is a traditional way to get people to identify themselves, thus generating a lead. The mail package should concentrate on the free offer, not on the product or service. If the offer has *perceived* value to the respondent, they will ask for the item. Now you have a name. It is up to the salesperson, from that point on, to get the respondent interested in the product.

Write the right letter to the right audience. Short for business and long for consumer is a good rule of thumb. But, in the last analysis, the letter should be as long as it takes to say what you have to say!

WHY WRITE THE LETTER YOU DO NOT HAVE TO WRITE

Once one of my clients wrote me a short, but to the point letter expressing his appreciation for our successful direct marketing efforts on his behalf. He cited cold, hard figures that were favorable beyond even our expectations—and he sent a copy of his letter to the president of my corporation.

I don't know about you, but I don't get many letters like that. Not that I don't think we are deserving (doesn't everyone think they deserve more credit than they get?). But people just don't take time to write the letter "you don't have to write."

Maybe my client really knows more about direct mail than I do.

In savoring this very special letter, I mentally dissected it and found it encompassed seven rules to follow when writing the letter you don't have to write. Believe it or not, this type of a letter is often harder to write than a regular letter. Here are the major points to remember:

1.   *Write the letter promptly.*   As soon as you have the urge, idea, and/or data necessary, write it. The closer your reply is to the event or fact that provides the opportunity for the letter to be written, the greater the impact it will have. Write when it's *news*. And news is always *now*.

2.   *Carbon the right people.*   How to decide? Think of it from the point of view of the recipient. Who would they like to see share the same good news? Don't hesitate to carbon the president of the company. As president of our company, nothing gives me greater pleasure than receiving a letter that praises one of our 104 employees because they did something special. Not only does it make me feel good, but it gives me a chance to add a note and pass it on to the individual—with my compliments added.

3.   *Don't get flowery.*   Come to the point quickly—make your statement. If you ramble on and on, the impact of the deed is lost; the reader, and those carboned, will not believe all the flowery talk (and suspect that you have some ulterior motive) or conclude you don't know how to write a letter.

4.   *Use hard facts and/or numbers to support the praise.*   The higher we go in management, the more the universal language becomes numbers. Why not use numbers and facts to add credibility to your message?

5.   *Don't write with an ulterior motive.*   The letter you don't have to write must be sincere. If you have an ulterior motive, you have a good chance of being discovered. The backlash will do more harm than good. Don't write it.

6.   *Above all, sound sincere.*   One sincere sentence is worth a thousand flowery words.

7. *Speak on behalf of others you work with.* This automatically increases the impact or meaningfulness of the praise, compliment, and thanks. Others in your organization will say, "Gee, I wish I'd written that. But, I'm glad they included me."

Perhaps I should tell you the ripple effect this letter had on our company. First, I xeroxed a copy and gave it to my assistant with an added note: "Thanks to you," for she was largely responsible for the success that prompted the letter. She was walking on air all day and has the letter pinned to her wall. Naturally, I showed it to my partner (I've got to remind him that I'm doing my share!). Of course, I read it to all who worked on the account. Afterwards, two of them came to me with new, good ideas on how we might do an even better job for this client. The power of praise to motivate is awesome. Finally, there was a feeling of closeness at the next meeting with the client that had never existed before. Result: One of our most productive sessions.

I've definitely concluded that my client knows how to harness the power of direct mail.

WHY COUPONS SHOULD LOOK LIKE COUPONS

Please don't get me wrong. I really don't hate all art directors! I just hate art directors who mess around with coupons in space ads.

You've seen them: coupons that are sideways, coupons that are triangular, coupons that are in the middle of the page. I even saw one once that was on the top of a page.

They may look pretty, and they may win art awards—the problem is that most hard numbers show that they do not work at the cash register.

You see, the public has been conditioned since birth as to what a coupon ad should look like. Coupons follow certain basic rules:

1. *It looks like a coupon.*   That means that it is rectangular in shape, the way most coupons look.

2. *It looks like it has value.*   You have seen the bond-type borders. These tend to subconsciously enhance the value of the coupon to the reader. Although it has no intrinsic value, it just looks more valuable.

3. *It has dash marks all around it.*   Some art directors go for a solid rectangular line around the coupon rather than a dotted line. I have never seen any research that says which is the best. But, if I had to make a guess, the dotted line tends to subconsciously direct the reader towards cutting or tearing it out.

4. *The coupon is always in the lower right-hand corner.*   There is a very practical reason for this. Readers do not like to tear a page of a publication apart, not even a daily paper. But, they have been trained not to mind tearing out a little corner of something. This means that when you are running a space ad, your media department must request "right-hand page to accommodate coupon." If the ad is smaller than a full page, you will also want to request "outside position."

I have heard others say that since there is a shortage of right-hand pages, you might get better position if you design your page as a left-hand page, with the coupon in the lower left outside position. This might seem a small point, but I suspect that response might fall off because most people are right-handed. Do the test yourself—see how much easier it is to tear out a right-handed outside coupon than a left-handed outside coupon.

Since very few people run left-handed coupons, it has saved the magazine and newspaper industry a considerable amount of trouble as back-to-back coupons are eliminated. In one column or less ads, especially in mail order sections of publications, this problem cannot be avoided. This leads to an important concept in our next point.

5. *Consider no coupon at all.* A far better suggestion than altering the traditional-looking coupon is to consider doing a layout with no coupon at all. Perhaps the best continuing examples are ads that appear in airline magazines, *The Wall Street Journal,* and other upper-income publications regularly.

Note that more and more small space ads, especially in the mail order sections of magazines, do not use coupons. There are some very good reasons for this. One is that many publications have a high pass-on readership, and the advertiser does not want to risk having the first reader tear out the coupon so none of the other readers have a chance to respond. While this is mathematically a small problem, it does exist.

There doesn't seem to be a drop-off in the response rate of couponless ads. About the worst thing that happens is incomplete address information. When the coupon fails to remind you to list your apartment number, you may forget it. This may hurt deliverability.

I personally feel that one of the reasons response does not seem to drop if a coupon is not included in a mail order ad has to do with creating a mail order feel. Quite simply, one of the purposes of coupons is to make the advertisement look like a mail order ad. In other words, it is a very good way to quickly put in the reader's mind, as they skip through the publication, that here is something you send for. Small space advertisers accomplish the coupon effect by the fact that their ads appear in the mail order section of a publication, so everyone knows it is a mail order ad.

So you see, a standard, typical-looking coupon has two purposes in a mail order space advertisement. First, it obviously makes an easy and accurate device to respond. Second, it gives the ad an appearance of a mail order advertisement.

Coupons in Mailing Pieces

Up to now I have been talking about space advertising. Do these same rules apply to direct mail pieces?

The principles do, but the execution does not. There is one huge advantage that a mailing package has over space when it comes to couponing: the coupon can become an entirely separate piece of paper in the mailing package—the response card. Or, as we say in the trade, the BRC, business reply card.

Because you can include the business reply card or envelope in your mailing, you eliminate a hurdle that space advertising faces. You eliminate the hassle a respondee must go through to find an envelope, address it and add postage. Convenience is one of the reasons that response is so much higher to direct mail offers.

Some horrible examples of direct mail I see are that there are simple space ads reproduced and inserted in an envelope. This is not direct mail, or at least not good direct mail. If you are going to the trouble of using an envelope, be sure to take advantage of the direct mail capability, expensive as it is, and have your response vehicle a separate item, or certainly easily detachable from a letter. Make it easy for the reader to respond.

If you are an art director, don't try to reinvent the wheel. Don't let your instinctive desire to create revolutionary new graphic concepts dictate what you do. Look through publications and see what other mail order advertisers are doing, especially the ones that repeat their ad time after time. Don't try to win awards. Follow direct mail and mail order basics. In advertising that doesn't solicit a direct response, you can get away with murder.

Remember, in direct mail and mail order there is a cash register looking over your shoulder every time!

THE SIMPLER AND SHORTER, THE BETTER

Millions of dollars in sales have been lost and millions of leads have never surfaced because of a problem that the advertising community often fails to remember. Maybe this is one area where advertising professionals are too close to the forest to see the trees.

Quite simply, the advertising community, who are *readers*, are deciding what will appeal to the public, who are *nonreaders*. Advertising experts write and edit based on their own experiences and environment. For most direct mail and mail order audiences, this is an unfortunate trap.

Advertising copywriters read a great deal. Most writers like long sentences, paragraphs, and words. They are comfortable with them and, in their minds, this more complex approach reflects a degree of sophistication of their writing art. Most of us in advertising and business who have the editorial or approval of advertising responsibility like to read. Many of us are comfortable with long sentences, paragraphs, and words. Unfortunately, most readers are not!

Today's market grew up on television, a medium that teaches a passive form of reading. Television turns the page for you. You don't force yourself to read ahead. As a result, today's consumers are a different animal than most of us old-timers. They are lazy readers.

This is especially important because direct mail is a medium that requires a great deal of reading.

Today's Consumer Hates Reading

Perhaps 10% of the population does 90% of the *voluntary* reading. There are a great deal of magazine subscribers. But it is a hard-core subscribing to several magazines. How many of us really read all that we subscribe to? Look at the pictures? Yes. Scan? Yes. But read? No. Many of our publications are defined within our industry as coffee table pieces, and that is where they stay. In many publications, readers read the ads and the pictures only.

Direct Mail's Curse

Magazine and newspaper advertisers have the safety of knowing that their audience reads. If they didn't, they wouldn't subscribe.

Direct mail goes to lists. With most of those lists, except books and subscriber lists, the degree of reading interest and reading skill is unknown. A list is selected because of someone's job title or because of a purchase or a donation. It is not based upon reading habits. So the direct mail writer has a much stronger reason to write simply and carefully to his audience, since many prospects on the mailing list are nonreaders.

Force the Prospect to Read

That is exactly what the direct mail advertisers must do. You must bribe the prospect to read what you want the reader to read, comprehend, and retain. There is a very easy way to do this. You need remember but one word—benefits. Yes, benefits are like the rabbit on the dog track or the carrot on the stick. Benefits keep the prospect plowing through all the way to the end and taking the action you wish them to take.

How to Keep Your Reader Reading

Or, should I say, how to get your reader to read enough to do what you want them to do: respond with an order, a lead, or a donation. Here are a few basics that we have found helpful.

1. *Benefit subheads.*   Your copy should be loaded with benefits. Make them stand out. As soon as a reader is made aware of one, and comprehends it, another should appear.

There is a second reason for benefit subheads. The scanning reader sees enough benefits scanning that he or she goes back and reads copy in depth.

2. *Simple words and sentences.*   If you want a rude awakening, take your copy to the entrance of a typical supermarket and ask shoppers to tell you what their understanding is of what they read. You will find each one giving you a different interpretation. There is only one interpretation you want. Keep revising copy until you get the same answer, or understanding, every time.

3. *Emotional words.*   Words like free, new, save, you, easy, low cost, big savings are easily understood. Moreover, they keep the reader reading. Remember, you have to keep the reader reading and understanding long enough to get action.

4. *Personalization.*   Talk about me. Mention my name. Talk about my needs. Talk about my benefits. In short, what is in it for me? That is what personalized "computer" letters do. If you don't have the volume for a computer letter, use general words like "you" and "yours," and "I" and "we."

5. *Instant good copy.*   The very best way to learn how to execute these important elements is *not* to write. Describe what you want to say *verbally* to someone who knows nothing of your product or service. Sell them! Sell them by talking, not writing.

Most people use shorter words and sentences when they talk. You will use short words and sentences too.

All direct mail and mail order copywriters should have retail or door-to-door selling experience. Salespeople have learned how to sell. They know short, simple, direct statements work. They also find out that one should never overestimate the educational and comprehension level of the American public. They learn, first-hand, what a short attention span the public has.

If you haven't sold, take your current copy to your nearby supermarket today and give it a real consumer test. You'll either start over, realize that you should do some selling on the side, or go into sales and turn out to be one sensational salesperson. In any case, you will be a better communicator!

PERCEPTION: HOW FAR CAN YOU GO?

Perhaps the most important word in direct marketing is "perception."

To put it succinctly, direct marketing, by definition, means marketing without the involvement of a store. That means you can't really see, touch, smell, squeeze, listen, try on, shake, or rattle. Moreover, no salesperson is around to answer questions, discuss, or actually sell you. That means it's up to your *perception* as to what it takes to generate the sale, which puts a huge burden on perception. It has to do a great deal. That leads to both problems and opportunities. If you don't develop a strong perception, you'll never properly communicate, and probably never make a sale.

If you oversell with your perception, you may be over-promising to such an extent that the reader will be greatly disappointed with what is received, and your return rates may soar. You might lose a lot of customers who never bother to return the items. They just decide that they won't do business with you again because they perceive you will over-promise on everything. For many years this was a problem with a large segment of the mail order industry.

Here are some thoughts on how to judge just how far to go on perception.

1. *Pretend you are a retail salesperson.* In fact, every copywriter should, at some time in their career, have been a retail salesperson. You quickly learn how far you can go in selling, and how quickly a customer turns you off if you go over the edge. Just as important, you learn how helpful selling really is to close a sale—so you realize the need for selling. You also learn how really basic and straightforward the customer's questions usually are.

2. *Perception of need is based on perceived benefits.* It is not based on features. Benefits fill needs more emotionally than features. Notice how a good salesperson says, "That really does something for you!" rather than "It's got over 50 pleats."

3. *Paint imaginary pictures with words.* But they must be *believable* pictures. Phrases like "you'll feel like a queen," "actually can help you get ahead," or "can save you money" will be better received than "you'll look like a famous Hollywood beauty queen," "go to the top of the class," or "the most important savings of your life."

4. *Talk about what the picture doesn't show.* One picture may be worth a thousand words, but in reality you can't possibly picture all the important benefits a product affords. Certainly, you want the picture to reinforce the copy, but you should also make sure the copy goes beyond the pictures if there are other important benefits.

5.   *Graphically provide the right picture frame.*   If you are selling quality, the "frame" or background to your picture must exude quality. Don't go overboard. If the product looks silly in a situation, you might not be doing yourself any good. The one exception is women's clothing where anything seems to go.

If your product is on sale, the graphics and copy approach should look like sale advertising. One of the mistakes people frequently make is to portray their sale in a sterile atmosphere, as if they are embarrassed to even be having a sale. If you hide it, you might as well not even have one.

6.   *Stick with the truth but graphically edit.*   This is another way of saying "put your best foot forward." That is fine as long as it is a real foot. The best way is to zoom in on the good features and crop out the bad features. If your product looks great on a straight front shot but comes off poorly with side shots, then photograph it straight on.

7.   *Perception works in many areas of communication.* Perception is important in testimonials. The reader has to perceive that the person giving the testimonial is qualified. Using phrases like "noted authority on" helps.

The reader has to perceive that you will care about them as an individual, and they won't get lost in the shuffle. That is why personal letters are important in mail packages and catalogs.

Perception is also important to the overall look of your mailing. That means if you want to create the perception of quality, your look is quality. If you want to look like a discount house, you look like a discount house.

In fund-raising, you don't want to look too high quality or people will perceive that you don't really need any money.

Always think perception.

MYTHS ABOUT GRAPHICS

Before the resurgence of direct mail, graphics tended to dominate the scene. Pretty ads make art directors and graphics specialists look good. Besides, it's easier to sell a client with prettier ads.

In direct marketing, catalogs that were graphically dynamic worked in some cases and not in others. In direct mail, beautiful packages seem to win out less times than most people expect. While graphics-dominated programs are winning awards, there are huge armies of marketers who are using simple, straightforward, plain communications and winning the real battle of higher response, larger orders, lower costs, and, thus, higher profits.

The ideal is a balance. There are several reasons expensive graphics fail. Let's look at some of them:

1. *Cost.* Beautiful, bleed, four-color graphic mailing packages cost a bundle. Not only is color more expensive, but these complex packages usually have more pages, and thus a greater creative, paper, and printing cost. These costs are compounded when they are placed against smaller mailings. Creative costs are one-time costs. No matter how many pieces you mail, the copywriting, layout design, production paste-up, typesetting, photography, and color separations are all fixed.

As an example, a complex four-color mailing package could cost $20,000 for all the above mentioned items. Let's say we have two mailings. One is a 10,000 piece mailing and the other is a 1,000,000 piece mailing. These one-time costs add $2000 per thousand pieces if mailed to the small mailing, while only $20 per thousand when mailed to the large mailing.

Now, let's say we could do the creative in a simple way for one-fourth that amount, or $5000. And, let's assume our paper, printing, and postage to be $300/per thousand on the larger mailing and $500/per thousand on the smaller mailing. The difference is in the volume savings on printing and paper.

Now let us look at our comparison of the greater impact of expensive graphics and creative costs against a small mailing versus a large mailing.

Table 1

| | Small Mailing 10,000 | | Large Mailing 1,000,000 | |
	$20,000 Creative	$5,000 Creative	$20,000 Creative	$5,000 Creative
Paper/print/M	$ 500	$ 500	$300	$300
Creative cost/M	2,000	500	20	5
Mailing cost/M	$2,500	$1,000	$320	$305

Going from $5,000 to $20,000 in creative costs causes a 150% increase in package cost on a 10,000 piece mailing, and only a 5% increase on a 1,000,000 mailing.

Clearly, a heavy creative cost against a small mailing presents an enormous burden to pay for itself. On large mailings, expensive creative is easily absorbed. The more expensive creative has to generate a 150% increase in response rates on a small mailing and only a 5% increase on a larger mailing.

2. *Graphics can detract from copy message.*   There are two aspects here—fancy type and reverse type.

Fancy type faces, with exotic serifs (that's the tail or foot on a letter character) or uncommon design, tend to hurt readership. Since graphics are supposed to bring the reader to the message, as well as support the message, you will find this difficult to accomplish if graphics detract.

The second detraction is reverse type. Sophisticated tests have shown that if you use reverse type in the body text of your catalog, response rates will drop about 15%. Further, reverse type against a color background forces you to change all four-color plates if you wish to change copy or have different versions of the copy with the same graphics. That means about four times the cost.

3. *Picture captions are essential.* Pictures are like Rorschach ink blots. Everyone sees something different. Your chance of communicating what you want to communicate is greatly enhanced if you write the caption first, giving your message, and then select a photo or illustration to support your caption.

The whole purpose is defeated if the art director places the caption away from the picture. We sometimes forget that the caption is more important than the graphics.

4. *Color.* Full color or process color gets a subjective answer when trying to determine what is best. So many people see colors in a different way, or not at all.

The biggest common denominator we've found about color is the difference of perception between males and females. To me, color is usually minimally important. To women, color is of vital importance.

It makes sense to have projects involving color that are directed more toward a female audience be designed by women and edited by women. The same argument can be made for men—that men should create and review the graphics and advertising designed for men.

All of this is not to say that graphics don't have an important place. It is to say that graphics must be kept in perspective.

Almost every time we test a plain envelope with a teaser, plus a letter, plus a reply card, the tests show that on a cost efficient basis, the simpler, the more efficient.

WHY SIMPLICITY WORKS

Beauty is simplicity. I wish I could remember who said that. Whoever it was, I'm sure they came up with it after analyzing direct mail results.

Year after year, the simpler packages seem to outpull the fancy, screaming, art-award generating, so called high-impact direct mail pieces.

Why do so many advertisers feel that a pop-up, four panel fold-out, extensive four-color, lots of mailing pieces, large sizes, odd sizes, and so on will do a better job?

The reason many people get off the track can be found at this very point. What is the job? What is a better job? Objectives are usually increased awareness, leads, or sales. Thus, a better job translates to better awareness, more and better leads, and more sales. But, alas, direct mail is usually too expensive a medium to use for awareness. Television, newspapers, radio, and magazines are much less expensive.

Direct mail must sell or generate leads. We don't care how many people remember our advertising, or how much they remember. We care about how many sales dollars are generated per dollar of advertising or promotion expenditure.

Fortunately, what is mailed in direct response can be measured. Time after time the direct, personal, simple approach generates more dollars per dollars spent.

So it pays to make it simple. That's the good news. The bad news is it takes a greater creative and marketing effort to be simple.

Steps to Simplicity

1. *Make sure each added increment more than pays its way.* If you add four pages on an eight-page catalog, will you get at least

a 25% increase in sales? (Your costs for postage and list will probably not go up, so a 50% increase in paper, print, and creative efforts probably leads to a 25% increase in total cost.) If you add a brochure to a letter, does it pay for itself? Test and measure the incremental difference.

2. *Use words that are logical and easy to understand.* Speaking in straightforward, simple language creates better comprehension. Fancy vocabulary and long sentences seem to appeal only to educators. Nobody is going to the dictionary to look up the meaning of a word.

3. *Use graphics to simplify.* If you have a complex application form, use tints, blocks, and screens to set the elements apart. Then use color, A-B-C or 1-2-3, to further simplify. Simplified applications pull better.

4. *Match your simplicity with a simple typeface.* Some typefaces look fancy, and fancy often gets confused with complicated. Small type often looks more complicated. Worst of all, the use of several different typefaces makes simplicity impossible to achieve. Since most of the world doesn't like to read, we'd better make it inviting and easy to read.

5. *Break up large blocks of copy.* On the surface, one would expect that a long column of unbroken type, with no indents, no underlines, and very few paragraphs, would be clean and neat from a graphics point of view.

Unfortunately, the eye tells the brain the opposite. The very mass of copy will appear to be too formidable a task to read. The eye looks with favor on typeset material that doesn't look too long, or where major points are emphasized so that key points will be picked up in skip reading. The public is lazy.

6. *Reduce the information you need.* Short response forms will out-pull long ones. Sometimes we let lawyers or senior executives get in the way and ruin a simple response device. However, lawyers are often the key to simplicity. Finding the right

kind of lawyer in a corporation who says, "You can't do this, but here is a way you might achieve your objectives," is worth his or her weight in gold. Ask them how you can simplify order forms, agreements, and so on.

7.   *Bury the boiler plate.*   It is often legally acceptable simply to state above a required signature: "I agree to abide by the terms and conditions on the reverse side . . . " then bury all the boiler plate on the reverse side.

8.   *Use photos or illustrations only if they support a copy point.* Color separations are expensive. Photographers and models are expensive. If they make sense, they will more than pay for themselves. If they are unnecessarily added, they can drown the project in excess cost.

If you can just do half of these eight steps, you will be on your way to simpler, more effective mailing packages.

"ONLY READ THIS IF YOU HAVE DECIDED NOT TO TAKE ADVANTAGE OF THIS FABULOUS OFFER"

More often than not, that is how a "lift" letter starts out. You've seen hundreds. They are the little piece of folded paper that falls out of a mailing package and usually has the above words hand-written in blue ink. Lift letters work.

They almost always more than pay for themselves. They *lift* response rates. And, since they don't cost much, they don't have to lift very much.

Before we tackle the question of why lift letters work, we need to study the rules that have been developed over the years and that continue to prevail. There are many variations of lift letters.

"ONLY READ THIS IF YOU'VE DECIDED TO BUY!"

You can bet that the nonbuyers are going to read this to see what they are missing.

"COMPARE THESE FIGURES"

This is another offshoot, where the deal being offered is far better than what the competition offers—so the difference is really meaningful.

"OUR OFFER IS ABOUT TO END. DON'T BE LEFT BEHIND."

This headline feeds on the human desire never to be left out on a good thing.

"READ WHAT ONE OF THE WORLD'S LEADING EXPERTS HAS TO SAY."

People like to feel confident that they are making the right selection. If an expert says it's right, that's good enough for me.

The alternatives are endless.

The conclusion we can draw is that lift letters truly lift response because they provide a dramatic way to make a very important point, and do so in the personal format of a letter.

The dramatic way is really dramatic. Think about it. Because of the handwriting, unique size, and hidden answer, the presentation within the mail package really is dramatic.

Lift letters seem to be used most when the other parts of the mailing package really aren't very dramatic. Lift letters aren't used with gorgeous four-color catalogs. Next, because they are small, they limit themselves to one point. Communicated alone, that points stands out. The fact that the format is a letter, and the mailing package, as a whole, is also a letter, keeps the format and flow of the package intact.

One of the rules of lift letters is that they should come from someone who is a higher authority, or a greater *perceived* authority, than the author of the basic letter. If the basic letter comes from the marketing director, the lift letter should come from a vice president. If the letter comes from the president or publisher, then the lift letter should come from some perceived authority outside of the organization making the offer. One of the reasons for this is that it allows for a new strong statement to be made. Or it offers to go into detail and prove a major point in the basic letter where there isn't space to go into detail.

Since we must have a greater authority, the lift letter must establish that greater authority immediately upon opening the lift letter. This can be done with a strong title on the stationery, or a first paragraph that comments on the authority.

It is usually a good idea to use a P.S. on a lift letter too. Just as a P.S. gets highest readership on a basic letter, it will get highest readership on a lift letter.

Why should lift letters be folded? They are folded because that is part of the suspense to the provocative handwritten headline. You've got to get involved, take a positive action and open it to get the answer.

Why are lift letters very small? They are small to look different from the rest of the mailing package. They stand out. By being small, the reader thinks it will just take a second to read. It does not look like a formidable document. This would be even more true in insurance mailing packages, which are formidable in their own right.

Why are the lift letter headlines or teasers handwritten rather than typed or printed? They are handwritten because it gives a personal flavor. And a personal flavor is what direct mail is all about. It is a personalized medium.

Another reason for the success of handwritten lift letter teasers is that the handwriting stands out from all the printed material in the mailing package.

There are certain places where you wouldn't use a lift letter. Self-mailers would be the most obvious example. Also, they make no sense with catalogs, because they would not be compatible with the catalog format. The catalog format is not a personal letter format.

Lift letters are not generally used in business mail either. The reason is that most business mail is designed to generate a lead. Letters are short, and a minimal amount of other items are included. A lift letter appearing here would be premature. The recipient does not yet know enough about the product or service being offered for the lift letter to support a major point or argument.

Lift letters do not have to be on expensive paper and do not have to look like the other stationery. It is simply an added note. As such, almost anything plain and decent will suffice.

Some people consider certificates and bonus coupons as lift letters. The purists would, perhaps, say that these items are "lifts" rather than lift letters. They, like letters, do lift. In fact, they are essential to an offer of that type, not an option.

In summary, never worry about whether adding a lift letter is worth it. Test and find out if you can afford to leave it out.

WHY YOU SHOULD NOT USE MAGAZINE OR NEWSPAPER ADS AS DIRECT MAIL

Newspaper and magazine ads shouldn't be used as direct mail pieces, and direct mail advertising shouldn't be made into print ads.

We often see ad reprints or dealer sheets stuffed into an envelope and mailed out by the smiling faces who love their ad and think it can be successful in other mediums.

Here are some of the reasons you should go back and start over, as far as flow and format are concerned. Keep your theme. Keep your basic artwork. Using existing materials is just fine. It is the way you use them that can cause you difficulties.

Here are some of the differences between direct mail and print advertising.

1.   *Reader exposure.*   In newspapers and magazines the reader must pass by your ad and see your entire message at one time. In direct mail, you are teased into the various parts. First you are teased from the envelope inside. Then you are pulled towards a brochure and then the response device. The reader gets a fuller story, but gets it piecemeal, perhaps not in the ideal sequence. So you must continue to attract the reader.

2.   A *full versus a short story.*   Obviously, you can go into greater detail in a mail piece than you can in a magazine. Direct mail, being a more experienced system of communication, must be utilized to the fullest to give it a chance to prove itself. One of its great advantages is telling the whole story.

The full story can include multiple pictures, a raft of testimonials, complete specifications, the many ways the product can be used, the multiplicity of ways it can be purchased, what add-on bells and whistles you can get and, most important of all, what benefits the reader will receive.

There are always multiple benefits. There are also many ways of saying the same benefit. It is better to talk too much benefit than too little.

3.   A *difference in headlines.*   A newspaper or magazine ad must have a headline to stop the reader and hold the advertisement together. There are also limitations on space for headlines,

as it must compete with the necessary copy, graphics, and coupon to give the balance.

In direct mail, there is rarely a problem on space for the headline. You can always write what you want to write.

Also mail headlines are often sequential, as they tease and carry you through the mailing package.

4. *Personalized letters.*   Above all, the great advantage of mail is the power, prestige, and stature that a personal letter has over any other form of printed advertising. Letters, by themselves, contain authority.

It is up to the copy and graphics people, who prepare letters and mailing packages, to take advantage of this extra lift a letter can give. If they don't, they are truly mailing out junk mail. The object is to come as close to a personally written, one-on-one letter as budget will allow.

Direct mail can also provide other elements that a space ad cannot. One is the involvement device. These are the token or stamp mailings that are best quickly explained as the "yes" or "no" tokens. "If you want this offer, attach the 'yes' token here." "If you only want to enter our sweepstakes, put the 'no' token here." There are great variations. Multiple subscription offers of magazine mailers allow you to paste down stamps for up to four magazines you wish to subscribe to. Catalogs, of course, have involvement devices in the order form you must fill out.

5. *Second class citizen treatment.*   If someone mails you an ad, you instantly know that something is wrong. You may say to yourself—"These people are too poor, too stupid, or don't care enough about me to send a letter."

The only time you can properly send an ad is when your letter refers to the ad. In other words, the ad serves, in a way, as a brochure. A problem arises quite often when you do this. The ad, as originally written, doesn't say the same thing you want it to say in relation to your letter and envelope copy. Worse yet, it often is repetitive where it shouldn't be.

And, finally, sending the letter probably won't save you as much money as you think. It doesn't save on postage, list cost, mailing operations, or the envelope. In fact, your envelope will probably have to be a large envelope or else your magazine or newspaper ad will be received all folded up. Not a very good way to present it.

Dealer sheets, by themselves, also make poor direct mail pieces. They are usually fact sheets. Sometimes they work if substituted for brochures.

It just makes sense to use each of the media you use properly.

WHY THERE IS A SHORTAGE OF GOOD DIRECT MARKETING COPYWRITERS

Over the years, I haven't found one in twenty advertising copy-writers who could write good direct mail or mail order copy. I never knew why. Was it lack of knowledge of direct mail/mail order principles? Was it lack of experience? We have an in-house creative staff of over 20 people. We are always looking for more. In testing some 20 free-lancers, very few of them could really do the job.

The guy sitting next to me at dinner came up with the answer. His name is Joe Karbo. He has done a lot of things, but he is known best for his best-seller, *The Lazy Man's Way to Riches*. He has sold 800,000 copies. At ten dollars a throw, that is eight mil-lion dollars. What he said made so much sense. Since he writes his own ads, he has the credibility to go with it!

Never hire a writer without selling experience. By selling, I mean door-to-door, retail, telephone, or whatever. But it must be one-to-one and with a large number of people, so the individual really gets a feel for what the public is really like. (As the psychiatrists say, after the first hundred there is very little difference.)

When you sell, you learn about people. What insecurities does the public have? How are men different from women? What pattern of susceptibility is there by age? What insecurities do people have when being sold? What major words or phrases turn them on? When do they turn on (or off!) to what you are saying? How does what they say differ from what they do? I could go on and on. I've never been in a selling situation where I didn't learn something.

Verbal Selling

Why are such great salesmen as Joe Crossman, Joe Karbo, and Clement Stone so good at copy? Because they have learned what works by selling verbally and getting reactions.

Many years ago, I was a very young account man at BBDO, working on the Rexall Drug Store account. At that time, it was one of the larger accounts in the United States. After a year on the job, I felt that I wasn't getting anywhere. There were lots of people ahead of me on the account. Everybody knew more than I did. Nobody would listen to what I had to say. One day I thought of a new strategy to get ahead. I would moonlight. I would work in a Rexall retail store. That job changed my thinking and gave my career a boost. Two years later I was hired by the client and put in charge of advertising/public relations for the entire corporation.

What happened? As I reflect back, two things. One, I got a first-hand viewpoint of what a customer was like. Hundreds of them. My preconceived notion of John Q. Public, developed behind a desk, was all wrong. Now I had a feel for what prospects and customers would and would not react to. I was totally unprepared for the second thing that happened. I suddenly became an expert and people listened to what I had to say because they were *not* moonlighting in a drug store.

Creating Awareness

Now how does all this relate to direct mail and mail order? General, or umbrella, advertising (most of what you see on television, radio, and in print) has the objective of creating *awareness*. It doesn't have to sell.

Direct mail and mail order must sell. They must get the response back, whether it is a lead card, a merchandise sale for cash, a donation, or a promise to buy. All are selling. While they may seem to be designed as soft sell, they are hard sell because direct response advertising must pay for itself. So it makes sense. Who knows better how to make advertising sell than someone who has sold!

TEN

VENDORS

WHY VENDORS ARE SO IMPORTANT

In direct mail, vendors become significantly more important to advertising and their agencies. Why? Because in space and broadcast, the media does the expensive part of the work. In magazines and newspapers, that means separations, printing, and distribution. Further, in direct mail, because of the many parts in the total mailing package—letter, envelope, reply envelope, brochure, and reply card—the project is much more complex. The effort behind one mailing package may be equal to the effort behind six space ads!

Therefore, the relationships with printing, envelope, computer printing, and lettershop vendors become especially important. They can make you look very, very good or very, very bad.

We regularly deal with about 50 vendors in doing 1000 direct mail packages annually. We'd like to share with you what we have learned.

1. *Select a vendor who has done work like yours.*   Ask for samples of what that vendor has done. If he or she can't come up with any, you know you are going to be training them rather than they training you. As I've said before, a good question to use to test direct mail knowledge is to ask the vendor to define BRE and BRC.

2. *Make sure your salesman or saleswoman has done work like yours.*   Ask the same question as that mentioned above. If the experience is weak, there is nothing wrong with asking the sales manager for an experienced contact. It may be the sales manager! You can bet the inexperienced individual will then attend courses or seminars to learn more.

3. *Work with smart people.*   Smart people, especially ones smarter than yourself, can help you enormously. They come up with the best and least expensive method, anticipate problems, don't let details drop through the cracks, and give you new ideas.

4. *How much quality do you really need?*   Quality costs more money. Is it worth it? Do the math. Will a 20% increase in total package costs, required to get your quality, get you 200% more responses? How did we compute that? Remember, product, price, creative theme, and list are all responsible for responses. Printing quality in most cases, we suggest, only accounts for about 10% of success. Or, in other words, would that same extra 20% in costs be more productive when applied to better lists or more pieces in the package?

5. *Document clearly.*   The original agreement, extras, changes, and delivery dates must be documented by both sides. Extras and changes can kill you. Many a printing quote has been made at or below cost but with sufficient profit generated from extras, changes, and rush charges.

6. *Quotes and invoices must be in the same language.*   Many vendors have not learned that if the final invoice is expressed in

the same terms as the quote, the invoice will be paid much more quickly. If they match exactly, fine. If there is a difference, and it is isolated, it is easier to approach and solve.

7. *Pretend you are the vendor.* You will get more for your money if you treat vendors fairly rather than squeeze. When to squeeze? Put yourself in the vendor's place and figure when squeezing makes sense.

8. *You should be paying for experience.* Why? Because it more than pays for itself—lowering your true costs for the hard goods you are purchasing. Your true cost is purchase price plus errors, late problems and hassle. If you buy low and have high problems, you are really purchasing high. If you are not demanding and receiving experience, you are not buying as inexpensively as you can.

There is no such thing as a free lunch, but there is the real world of late deliveries, errors, and a more expensive way of doing it.

CHECKLIST ON VENDORS

Getting the most does *not* mean squeezing the hardest. We in direct mail know this better than anyone because in direct mail you use many more vendors than in conventional advertising. Why? Because there are more parts to a mail package, and, in print media, the medium itself handles the printing and distribution aspects. In mail, you've got to do it.

We couldn't survive if we didn't develop a checklist to help us get the most out of vendors. "Most," in our terminology, is the best quality for the best price—considering service, vendor contribution, and promptness—all over the long pull. Our guide may help you.

1. *Select the right vendor.* Where it is practical, and you know what you want, do not use a middle-person. Go to the source of what you want—a type of organization that has dealt many times before with the spectrum of vendor choices you have.

Yellow Pages, associations, and other noncompetitive users like yourself, are the best sources for information. Don't be afraid to call. Most people like to help others.

2. *Make sure your vendor contact is experienced and intelligent.* Someone has to work with the newest salesperson on the block. But it doesn't have to be you. If you are stuck with "the salesperson assigned to your area" and it is not to your liking, call up the sales manager. Explain how important decisions he or she can help you make will be. I've yet to see a case yet where the brains of a vendor organization didn't pitch right in and help in any way they could.

3. *Explain what your objective is.* No, don't tell a vendor what you want. Tell them what you are trying to accomplish. Then tell them what you *think* you want. Then ask them for their comments.

You will be surprised how often a vendor has encountered your problem before. Perhaps over and over again. The vendor learns from each experience, and will usually be pleased to show you a better way to accomplish your objective, either by saving money, saving time, saving hassle, or increasing your impact. Listen carefully.

4. *A picture is worth a thousand words.* If you are in direct mail, you keep a "swipe file." That is the mailing packages of others. Pick one to show a format and/or to show the quality you expect. For printers, this will be just as important as the layout you provide. It lets the printer know what quality level is acceptable to you. High quality does not always mean the most profitable response to your mailing.

5. *Look at samples of a vendor's work.*   In selecting a printer, you want to see that what the firm has done before is similar to your needs. The last thing you want is to have a vendor experiment with you. If it is a list company, what do they have that works for a project and audience like yours? If it is a premium company, who can you check with for quality and delivery? If the vendor is in the creative or marketing area, ask them *why* they decided to do what they are showing you.

6. *Document your requests in writing carefully.*   Also review the documentation, or specifications, carefully with the vendor. Make sure there are no misunderstandings. Naturally, with each vendor, give the exact same specifications.

7. *Do not divide responsibilities between vendors.*   The best example of this pitfall is providing the paper stock to a printer. If you provided the paper and the finished job does not meet your specifications, the printer will blame the paper and the paper people will blame the printing job. You must give authority with responsibility.

8. *Visit a vendor's facility.*   Being on the wrong side of town, or lack of a Wilshire Boulevard address, is not important. What is inside a vendor's plant or office is important. Is it neat? Do the people look busy? Are they happy and do they seem to care? Does the place look organized? Do they have systems? All of these things are important.

9. *Figure a formula for bid selection.*   Price is important. Do some calculations to figure how important others aspects are. What is previous experience working with you worth? What risk can you afford on a low bidder who has never done this kind of a job?

10. *How far away is the home office?*   Given the choice between a firm whose branch is serving you versus the home office, take the home office. People are usually brighter, more special-

ized, and have more readily available data at the home office. Besides, the squeaky wheel gets the grease, and squeaks are pretty faint a thousand miles away.

11.   *Above all, be fair.*   Problems will happen, no matter what effort towards selection you make. Never go with a vendor on a one-shot basis. Long-term relationships will make both you and your vendor more money. Vendors must make profits too. If they are allowed to, they can and will spend more time on your projects. That alone will save you money in the form of new ideas, as well as time saved from explaining what you are trying to do to a new vendor each time.

If you are wrong, admit it and pay up. If the vendor is wrong, ask him what the solution is before you become too demanding. Then explain that you, too, want a long-term relationship.

12.   *When in doubt, put yourself in your vendor's shoes.*   In reality that says it all. You can bypass some of the above rules but never this one.

ELEVEN

TELEVISION

WHY INTERACTIVE TELEVISION IS SO SLOW TO DEVELOP

Interactive television is doomed to failure unless the proven principles of direct mail/mail order are followed.

Our definition of interactive television is simple: two-way communication between the home and television programming sources. It can be used for (1) entertainment, (2) information, or (3) to make a purchase of a product or a service. It is very expensive and very limited.

Because of the expense, the entertainment and information aspects won't be practical until the overhead cost of the equipment is amortized by the third use: the purchase of a product or service. That is direct marketing or in-home shopping.

The immediate future rests with in-home shopping.

Direct Mail Marketing Can Save Videotech

Major corporations are pouring millions of dollars into development of in-home shopping via TV. These people seem to have lost sight of the two keys to this fledgling industry's success—common sense and direct mail marketing methods.

These heavily bankrolled projects, whether here or abroad, all have one thing in common. Each claims development is coming along much slower than anticipated. Which, from the shareholder's point of view, means even more of the company's millions are being spent for development.

We should stop and take stock. The toy is too expensive.

Giant Misunderstandings

I was shocked the other day when a graduate business school student called and asked: "If in-home shopping is going to be so great, why has almost nothing happened in the last five years?"

Thinking he meant catalog sales, and having seen our direct marketing business grow over 500% in that period, I was perplexed. I explained that Sears's and Ward's catalogs have been providing in-home shopping for about a century, and the in-home shopping industry accounts for well over $100 billion in sales annually.

The student replied, "That's not in-home shopping. I'm talking about shopping by TV.!"

That student has a misconception of what in-home shopping really is. Many businesses make the same mistake by not looking at the opportunity from the shopper's point of view.

Consumers have already told us, through their purchases, that the present combination of telephone and mail order catalogs, along with credit cards, is great. Now another medium has been added—television. So what? What extra benefits will this provide for them?

Where Television Adds and Fails

Common sense would dictate that if "videotech" or "interactive" television is going to succeed, it must ask itself what it can add to the present mix of catalogs, telephone, and credit cards. It can provide the following:

1. Access to as many computer data banks that exist or could be developed (that is, all airline schedules, all real estate multiple listings, help-wanted ads, restaurant guides, books in print, and so on).

2. All the above information in "real time," with new information as well as current status (last-minute information on whether a house has been sold, a job already filled, or if a manufacturer is out of a certain size, color, and so forth).

3. Quick access to that small segment of the huge data universe that is of specific interest to you at that particular moment. You can access data more quickly than a library and certainly more quickly than going to the store, or having your fingers do the walking through the Yellow Pages.

On the other hand, television cannot:

1. Offer you instant (random) access to full-color pages of your favorite catalog.

2. Provide any of these services free.

What does this really mean from the viewer's point of view?

Choice Number One

Choice number one is a "living catalog" that shows, in full color, dresses modeled in action, tools being used, and so on. But there is one catch. All viewers must watch the same thing at the same time, like conventional television programming.

Television cannot accomplish the second aspect that presently makes in-home shopping so successful—a wider selection. The reader can go through a 64-page catalog at home in a few minutes and stop at items of interest. With a television catalog it would take hours, and you can't freeze frame when you want to look more closely.

TWELVE

FORMAT

THE IMPORTANCE OF THE BUSINESS REPLY CARD

Long live the BRC—the business reply card!

There are several schools of thought on which piece of a mailing package is the most important. Some argue the envelope, because if it is never opened nothing good can result. Some argue the letter with all its detailed selling messages, and some the brochure with all its excitement.

I lean toward the response card. Why? Because I think it does more all-around duty than any other part. For example, many people open up all mail, but a significant portion of those do what I call the "BRC peek." That is, without taking the contents out of the envelope, and with great manual dexterity, they read the lead-in to the business reply card while it's still in the envelope to see what the mailing is all about to determine if they want to really take it all out and get into it deeply.

The BRC (or sometimes the BRE—a business reply envelope

that has all the data on the flap, such as in fund-raising) is the one document, if it has been done properly, that tells the whole story and offer in one short paragraph, including the price or deal. If you don't get past the "BRC peek," you are nowhere. So it had better do its job well.

We've said before that each piece within a direct mail package must stand alone—and tell the whole story. This is especially true of the BRC. Very often the offer is of interest to the reader but action is put off. The only thing the reader saves is the BRC/BRE. If, at a later date, that document doesn't rekindle the flame or call-to-action of the original package, then the reader might never respond.

In addition to concisely restating the offer, a good BRC does several other things:

A BRC is *positive*. Almost any BRC you read says "Yes" as its first word, usually in big letters.

A BRC *calls the reader to action*. One of the biggest reasons mailers don't get response is lethargy. People just never get around to taking the action. The best time to get action is at the time of the first reading. After that it is all downhill. So a call to immediate action (or suffer dire results!) is of vital importance.

A BRC *is complete but simple*. As a writer of BRC copy, you first have to make it complete. Then, with good editing and the aid of graphics, struggle to make it simple. It is not easy. A good test is to show it to three people who know nothing about your product, service, or program. Be sure to ask them the leading question—"What don't you understand about this?" If they stumble anywhere, fix it.

A BRC *looks important and official*. If a BRC is almost barren of excitement and copy, it will receive the same result—barren response. It must look exciting.

A BRC *restates the guarantee*. Everyone likes to be reassured.

Be sure to tell them "no salesperson will call" or "your money back if not satisfied," or whatever is the case.

The last rule is as important as any. Ask yourself: When the response comes back to me can I properly fulfill the promise the way I want to? That means, can I quickly ship the merchandise or, with business mail, will my salespeople respond properly?

If you can't do the latter, go back to square one and start over!

THIRTEEN

TESTING

WHY SO MUCH TESTING?

The byword of direct mail and mail order is test, test, test. But the byword needs a qualification: test what is *meaningful*. If those in direct mail and mail order would spend the time and dollars they spend on testing trivia on testing what should be tested, there would be a lot more successful people in the industry today.

Unless you are one of the few really big mailers that send out millions of pieces a year, testing trivia will be trivial! These guidelines may be helpful.

1. *How much money will the test result save you?* If you test a bulk rate precancelled stamp versus an indicia and it pulls 5% better, but you only mail 10,000 pieces, the savings will be meaningless. Here is why: With a 2% response on a $19.95 item, you will get 10 more orders, or a total of $199.50 in additional sales. If your pretax profit is 20%, that is $39.90—hardly worth the effort.

2. *When you get the results, what can you do with them?* Take

the case of the company that tested First Class versus Bulk mail. They found Bulk mail worked better than First Class. But theirs was a timely newsletter-type advertising piece. The delay of the Bulk mail was unacceptable.

The following is a list of items that usually have so little effect on mailing results that testing them becomes a luxury too expensive to be affordable. While there are exceptions to each, the chances are that they will not be major factors.

Color of paper stock, texture of paper (quality), corner card versus flap return address, two-color versus three-color, glassine versus plain window envelope, separate pages letter versus front and back of sheet, blue versus black signature, metered versus Bulk rate indicia, one versus two colors on reply cards.

Rather than concern one's self about these factors individually, take the time to plan a package that utilizes what you think are the best combinations of items. This is a form of updating a mailing piece that is working very well for you.

Trivia is not exclusive to creative areas. Marketing trivia can be just as insignificant. When testing pricing, don't test $18.95 versus $19.95. More than a few mailers have been surprised how far they can go up and lose so few sales that they still increase total profit. If you only go up a little, you'll never know how far you could have gone.

List selection and segmentation can involve trivia too. If you are using one of the mass lists, such as a telephone, auto, or residence list, you have the opportunity to select on the basis of a dozen or more census tract figures. Testing small variations, such as income levels of $10,000 versus $8000, gives you too narrow a difference. At the same time, a single versus multiple family dwelling unit test could have a far greater effect in terms of both the number of names available and response rates.

There are at least 200 factors that affect the success or failure of any mailing. Your best judge is common sense. When I get carried away with "overtesting," I put the numbers to what I'm doing to see how much influence the factor has. Let's take one graphic-type trivia item. If list/audience factor and marketing factor (who you are, what you offer, and how much it costs) account for 80% of success or failure, that leaves creative with 20%. If graphics are half of creative, that is 10%. If there are ten graphic factors involved and I am concerned about only one, that means my factor in question is really only 1% of the package. Not only that, we would find the statistical variation of the result larger than the effect of the factor itself. Back to basics—themes, prices, and targeted lists.

WHY CODING IS SO IMPORTANT

It is easier to improve direct mail and mail order efficiency by use of proper coding than just about anything else. It should be a simple thing to do. As they say, "When everything else fails, follow directions!"

We all know we code to find out what works. By coding we can compare lists, copy inserts, media, mail or publication date, price, deals, enclosures, headlines, themes, and more.

The real question is what should be coded and how should it be done. Let's set some rules:

1.   *Code only if you can do something with the results—either good or bad.*   Coding can add extra expense, such as media or list charges, count reports, supervision, and a mismatch of overs and shorts that increase printing costs. If you can't do something about results, don't bother.

2. *You don't need coding data back on 100% of your orders or replies.* Catalogs are a good example. For most catalogs, the only practical place for coding data is on the address label. Because order forms are generally inside the catalog, the customer is asked to remove the peel-off label and affix it to the order form inside. Many customers don't bother. That should not discourage you because what you are looking for is *relative* results—not the total response rate, but how different segments relate to each other. Thus those that failed to affix the label would be expected to respond in the same proportion as those who did.

3. *For most mailings, you've got to use a window envelope to retrieve coded orders or replies.* The code must be on the label to retrieve it; it must be affixed to the reply card. Thus a window envelope must be used to show the label attached to the response card. Self-mailers can use die-cut formats.

4. *Know your universe before you start.* To tabulate, you must know the universe mailed or circulation advertised. Receiving 410 responses from a 10,000 mailing is not as good as 250 responses from a 4000 mailing. Remember, in direct mail, it is *not* the quantity printed or number of labels ordered that counts. It is the number actually mailed. In space you must know your circulation.

5. *You must know the size of segments mailed.* When using the mails, you may often order and test segments of a list. For example, if you are mailing a list that includes names captured over a 3-year period, you need to code each year and know how many you mailed from each year, not just the total for all years. When you order your lists, be sure to order counts on all segments included.

6. *Keep records before it is too late to change.* Be sure to list all lists, sublists, publications, copy tests, marketing tests, and so on before you mail. After each item, list the total number ordered or circulation. Assign the code letter or number. At a quick glance

you will see if you're missing anything, or have used a symbol more than once.

7. *Stay away from the letters "o" and "i."* Because they look like zero and one, misuse can cloud your results.

8. *Confirm your coding orders.* Make sure you look at each list supplied to confirm your order was executed properly. For space advertising, make sure you get tear sheets for each ad. Then check off against your preadvertising coding sheet (described in paragraph six).

9. *If you've coded incorrectly or forgot to code, don't give up.* In space ads you can look at the back of the coupon and determine which publication or issue each coupon is from. Once we reconstructed a test of all *Wall Street Journal* editions by securing sample copies of each edition. We were lucky—the back of each of our coupons was different.

10. *If you are dropping mail on different dates, be sure to code each drop differently.* Different drop dates themselves can be a difference. When doing the fine tuning of your analysis, you may want to check data from different drop dates.

11. *Have someone else look over your coding plans.* Sometimes you can be too close to the trees to see the forest. Coding mistakes are often very subtle. The open mind of someone not overly familiar will often find mistakes. It is just like proofreading.

12. *Code parts of your package.* If you are doing a mailing that has two or more parts—letter, response card, envelope, and/or brochure changes—remember to code each. This is a great help to your mailing house.

Coding seems so simple. But how often, amidst a sea of papers deep in response analysis, have each of us said, "If only I had coded that segment." It is bound to happen sometimes, but you can certainly reduce how often it will happen by following these directions, and providing that direct marketing edge.

USE DIRECT MARKETING
FOR PRERESEARCH

It's pretty scary. The product development program is budgeted in the millions. As to how well the marketplace will accept it, all that is known are the results from preresearch of what a few people say they *might* do.

What if you could find what people *did do*—beforehand? Why not make part of your preresearch program a mail order test? Mail order is unique. It deals with what people actually spent. "What if" research is no match for "cash-on-the-barrelhead" testing. Confidence levels could soar.

Let's take a hypothetical case. You have developed two bars of soap with distinct aromas. You also have two distinctly different copy approaches for each soap. What combination yields the greatest sales?

You have a four-way direct mail test. Select a mailing list that is a cross-section of your market. Divide that list in four equal parts on an "Nth" name basis.

Develop four different mailing packages, coupon inserts or newspaper ads. Aroma A, Copy A; Aroma B, Copy A; Aroma A, Copy B; and Aroma B, Copy B. If you use print, select a four-way test combination.

Rather than direct your prospects to a store to purchase the product, you include a coupon with your direct mail or in your ad, properly coded. They must send in their money to buy the soap. Mail all four versions simultaneously.

What you will *not* learn is how successful each is. But what you will learn is how successful each of the four segments is *in relation* to each other! In other words, which is the best of the four combinations.

People will have paid money to purchase, and therefore will

give you a far more meaningful answer than preresearch. There are several benefits to this "cash-on-the-barrelhead" type testing.

- *Speed.* Split run newspaper ads can be done on a few days' notice with short closing times. In some cases, answers are available in days as opposed to weeks.
- *No confusion with retailers.* Since this program can be executed under another product and/or manufacturer name, and because the purchase cycle bypasses the retailer and your sales force, you can test to your heart's content.
- *The cost of testing is low.* The cost of a several thousand mailing or a split run space ad test can be less than the cost of a focus group program.
- *The "Didn't Buy" segment can be probed.* An important part of research is to find the stumbling blocks as to why people didn't buy. You have the phone numbers included on your mailing list and can do phone, mail, or in-person interviews with them.
- *Matching profiles.* Since the mailings were at random, you can compare the demographics of the "Didn't Buy" group with the "Did Buy" group. That will help in media selection and copywriting.
- *The competition will be kept in the dark.* Using another name, no one will know what you are up to. Secrecy is greater with mail because less people will see your ad, and clipping services do not audit mail.
- *No packaging required.* You can send out the different versions in a jiffy bag because the sale has already been made. This reduces development costs.

As an aside, you can hype your response rate and not adversely affect what you are testing. Remember, we are not measuring the depth of response. We are doing comparative testing. So you can really lower the price to get more responses. Just lower all segments equally.

These testing opportunities are not limited to products. They can be used to find which political appeals generate the most interest (and money!). They can also be used to determine how simple or complex the sale of a service (such as financial services) must be. Furthermore, they can be used to test personalities for endorsements. The uses are endless.

It is not difficult to predict that almost every major advertiser will be in mail order without anybody ever knowing it. Are you keeping a step ahead?

FOURTEEN

EDITING

WHY SOME PEOPLE ARE BETTER EDITORS

An editor of direct marketing is, in my mind, defined as someone who has the responsibility for the execution of a direct marketing program.

Editors have many titles: account executive, account supervisor, product manager, advertising director, marketing director, and, in many cases, the president.

That means they must supervise the copywriters, art directors, printers, media specialists, and marketing specialists. They are responsible for the input to these people and the control, modification, or acceptance of the output.

There are several traits that good editors either are born with or acquire—or, as in most cases, a combination of both. Let's review some of the traits of those direct marketing editors I respect most.

Observance From the Reader's Point of View

They put themselves in the reader's mental set. To do that, they have determined who the advertising is directed toward and try to develop an awareness of that market's characteristics. These characteristics would include age, sex, income level, industry, job within the industry, and marital status. The hardest of all of these is sex because women and men think and react differently. Good editors require a person of the opposite sex to review the advertising if the advertising is directed toward the opposite sex.

They also must put themselves into the role and pretend to be buffeted by the various economic, social, and traditional elements that accompany this person's characteristics. They do this by thinking of acquaintances who meet these requirements and reflect how they react to similar situations. Where there are multiple audiences, the editor should do this exercise for each of them.

1. *Market needs.* Now that the audience has been pinpointed and profiled, we move on to that group's needs and wants.

2. *What are the benefits of the offer?* The benefits are what you are selling. So the good editor quickly relates the stated benefits to the perceived needs.

3. *Features.* What are the product or service features that enable the targeted readers to meet their needs?

The editor must also prioritize ad control. What are the important needs or wants? These must be able to be related to the product offered. The important ones are featured, the average ones are mentioned, and the small ones are, perhaps, omitted.

4. *Guarantee.* Is the guarantee reasonable? Is the guarantee meaningful? Will the typical targeted reader react positively to the guarantee?

5. *Is the offer simple?* Do I, as the reader, instantly understand it? Complex offers, choices, multiple options, and so on tend to confuse. As we have said elsewhere, confusion often results in the reader doing nothing.

6. *Is the order form simple and complete?* From the reader's point of view, the offer must not only be simple, but the response device must also be simple. Easy to read and fill out. Impossible to make mistakes with. Good editors often assume that if a reader can make a wrong choice, he or she usually will.

Completeness is important to the advertiser. If all the information has not been gathered that is necessary to fill the reader's order, then the advertiser must either take a chance he will be fulfilling the wrong item or enter into an expensive written or telephone dialogue with the consumer.

7. *Does the communication flow?* We have talked about many elements. The editor has the best chance to test the advertisement and see if it really does flow. Since he is not the writer or art director, he can read it more objectively—the way a typical reader might glance at it.

Years ago, a famous direct mail writer had an unusual opportunity. He was riding on a plane, sitting next to a total stranger who picked up the airline magazine and soon came to the writer's own ad. To make matters better, the stranger used the speed-reading technique of reading with his finger.

The writer watched out of the corner of his eye as the stranger stopped at his ad and started reading the three columns of copy. While the writer had visions of the reader continuing through, tearing out the coupon, and filling it out, no such luck was in store. Even more helpful was the fact that the reader continued halfway down the second column. He then stopped and turned the page. Something in the flow wasn't good enough to continue to hold the reader's attention.

Our friend, the writer, rushed home and looked at his ad. Sure enough, there was a block in the flow. The writer fixed the blockage and changed his ad. His response rate rose in future tests of the ad. The writer had really benefited more from this learning experience because, although he lost a sale, he received far more from future ads.

8. *Respect for costs.* More complex ads cost more money. As we have pointed out, the simpler advertisements tend to work more efficiently. If you have an advertisement that pulls 50% more but costs twice as much, you are losing.

A good editor develops a sense of cost at the outset of development of a mailing package, so that the mistakes are corrected before the major monies are expended.

9. *A sense of people.* A good editor will find changes are often necessary. It is human nature to be defensive when someone is critical of one's work. A good editor senses this and tries to work around the situation to the point where the change is the writer's or designer's idea.

People will always become more involved and do a better job on their own idea. Further, it is important that the people who must make the changes fully understand why the changes are being implemented. In that way, not only will their corrections be better, but they will be less likely to make the same mistake in the future.

10. *Anticipation.* Good editors anticipate. They anticipate the schedule, knowing the check points along the way that could indicate if the project is running late.

Good editors must also anticipate the reactions of other people who review and pass on the advertisement. This means arguments must be prepared beforehand to prevent the possible misdirection of further editing. It is especially important to direct marketing editing because top executives often have a very limited understanding of direct marketing.

11. *Common sense.* This is the most important trait of all, and no list of qualities of a good editor would be complete without it.

HOW TO EDIT

Most readers of this book are probably pretty smart. (Dare I say that taking time to read this book shows a certain amount of intelligence?) The problem is that you probably lack experience when it comes to direct mail and mail order.

Hang on, because by the time you get to the end of this you will be perceived as a "pro." Notice I said *perceived.* You want others—vendors, peers, subordinates, and certainly your boss— to think you know what you're doing in the world of direct marketing.

These few tips are guaranteed to work, because quite simply, direct marketing is a business of numbers. After 30 years of tabulating results, it all comes down to a pattern.

Before we start, let's make one assumption. You are the editor, the person who doesn't have to ideate and create. Let the direct marketing professionals do that. You just have to review, which is another way of saying keep the train on the track. So here are a few rules that will make you a good direct mail editor, or at least be perceived as one.

1. *Hire (or contract with) good direct marketing professionals to do your work.* The definition of a good direct marketing professional is one who knows more about lists, direct marketing media, and basic direct marketing principles, as well as the creative aspect. It took me several years to realize the primary *cause* of poor copy and graphics. It is usually not the communicative capability of a writer or art director. The problem in most instances is faulty

marketing and media. Unfortunately, most direct mail copywriters are not good marketing and media people.

2.   *Never say, "This is exactly what I want done."*   You are paying good money to creative people. If you've got it all figured out, you should be the direct mail copywriter or art director. Good ones make more money than editors! Most supervisors have an Achilles' heel. They are so engrossed in what they have to sell, they forget that they must think in terms of what the reader wants to buy.

3.   *Never apply magazine or newspaper advertising rules to direct mail or even a mail order space ad.*   In many ways, the rules for direct mail are 180 degrees opposite conventional advertising. Why? Direct mail is a three-dimensional medium. It is also one that works without editorial copy at its side, so it must create its own editorial. What works on a page ad usually doesn't work for a direct mail piece. Want to prove it to yourself? Just mail out a reprint of your latest space ad and see how much action you get! There is another reason to use direct response rules. They have been proven again and again. Remember, in direct response we get a coupon or phone call back. We learn what works.

4.   *Always put yourself in the frame of mind of the intended reader.*   If your audience is typically a dentist in Toledo, pretend you are a dentist in Toledo. If you can't, have someone else who can do the editing. When editing a mailing to women, I make sure that at least two women review the mailing or space ad.

5.   *Check the flow with a common sense approach.*   Now that you are a dentist in Toledo, start reading at the right place—the beginning. If it is a mailing package, the beginning is the outside envelope. (Remember, if it is a catalog the label is on the back, not the front. I've seen many a catalog whose back looked so bad I'm sure most were in the waste basket before the beautiful front cover was even seen.) Open the package and read the letter or whatever catches your fancy first. You'll be surprised at the dif-

ference between a package that hangs together and one that doesn't.

6. *Make sure that the layout and copy are reviewed in real life situations.*   Never look at a mail order space ad in the abstract. Put the layout inside the newspaper or magazine you propose to use and see how it does against the competition. For direct mail, make a dummy. Make sure that the letter is typed out on the letter layout. You'll be surprised what you'll learn.

7. *Don't nitpick.*   Battling over the copy is a waste of your time. If you must nitpick, do it where it counts. That is the media strategy—planning the basic marketing concepts. Remember that media and marketing together are *four times* more important than copy, headlines, graphics, type of paper, postage rate, and type style combined. Work on what is important.

There you have it. If you do all this, you will probably have done much more than many writers and art directors ever got around to doing. Thus you are fulfilling a real need in the development process. You'll probably find you are worth more than you are being paid, and sooner or later water will seek its own level.

DIRECT MAIL EDITOR'S CHECKLIST

If you are an advertiser using direct mail, and you are responsible for the development of a direct mail program, you are the editor. As such you must know what you're doing because most ad agencies have limited experience in direct mail.

The principles that work for general advertising do not usually apply to direct mail. Unfortunately, almost all the people who approve direct mail advertising have come up through the ranks of general advertising, and edit based on their experience in general adveritising—not direct mail experience.

Maybe these procedures will help.

- *Look at mail as your reader will.*   That means the letter is typed on the layout, folded in the envelope with all its enclosures. People who display advertising layouts in beautiful folders or styrofoam easels ought to be shot! As the appraiser, you should review it as the reader will (if it's a space ad, it should be in a newspaper or magazine). You'll also find out if the pieces fit together and flow correctly if you look at direct mail like your recipients do.
- *Keep foremost in your mind the primary objective.*   That doesn't mean, for example, getting a lead. It does mean getting someone to express enough interest and understanding to respond.
- *Does the number one benefit hit you between the eyes?* Readers react to benefits for them, not to features.
- *Does the number two benefit follow close behind?*   If one is good, two are better. (There is one exception. If you are lead generating, you may have several major points. In that case, you do one at a time in a series mailing.)
- *Does the mailing package flow?*   That may seem impossible with a mailing package that contains several elements: envelope, letter, lift letter, reply card, reply envelope, and brochure. There is a natural flow, from envelope to letter to brochure to response card.
- *Does the outside envelope encourage you to open it now?*   Usually a teaser line, or promise of a benefit are the most common devices. And graphics support these. Sometimes the corner card (the sender's logotype and address) is sufficient. The best example I can think of would be an envelope that says "Internal Revenue Service." Just try not opening that one!

Notice that I said *open now*. A call to action always gets better response.

- *Is the letter the first thing you see upon opening the package?* It should be. The letter is a cover letter. People are used to reading letters first. Subconsciously or consciously, they will go to the letter first. If the letter has a headline and the envelope has a teaser, they should flow from envelope to headline.

- *Does the letter discuss the reader's needs, product benefits, features, endorsement and how to respond?* There is no use talking about features until you have established a need and benefit in the reader's mind.

- *Do graphics support copy?* Graphics must improve communication. This means that sometimes the best graphics are no graphics. If you are writing a president, your letter must look like executive-to-executive correspondence. Excess graphics are often the reason junk mail earns its title.

On the other hand, if you are offering low-cost merchandise, you want to look like a sale.

- *Does the reply card tell the whole offer?* Sometimes the reply card is the only thing kept, pending perceived later response. When it is again picked up, the reader will have forgotten all those good selling points in your letter and brochure. The response card must be a reminder, so it repeats the benefits and essentials of the offer.

- *Is there a reason to act now?* The longer the wait, the less the chance of a reply. We call this the action device. It is the special benefit or offer for acting now.

- *Is it easy to reply?* If not, you will lose responses. If readers are confused, they will act as humans—they will do nothing.

- *Would you respond?* If you're true to yourself, you probably wouldn't. Immediately ask yourself why. Then figure out how that barrier could be eliminated.

NINE TIPS TO BEAT DIRECT MAIL MISTAKES

Nobody listens to their parents! I suspect that in business that would translate to nobody really listens to their immediate boss. Since I am not your boss, maybe you'll remember these nine tips on the biggest causes for mistakes in the mail order/direct mail world.

- *Make a dummy.* And put your letter in the window envelope dummy at the layout stage. A piece of mail is a complexity of items and sizes. There is nothing more embarrassing than several thousand brochures that won't fit in the envelope, or part of an illustration peeking through the envelope window.
- *Put your mail order newspaper ad layout in the newspaper.* And at the worst possible position. Chances are, that is where it will end up. Be prepared for the worst and make sure your ad stands out *anywhere*. Looking at an advertisement on a beautiful art board is not very realistic.
- *Specify either left- or right-hand page—outside.* Then, in your magazine and newspaper advertising, put your coupon on the appropriate side to be on the outside. Don't put the coupon in the middle. That gives you the worst of both worlds.

  When doing bind-in cards next to your ad, specify on your insertion order front or back half of book, so you know which way the card will fold—on top of your ad or away from it. Since you know how the coupon bind-in will look, you can design it properly. The upside of the bind-in card should *not* be the address side.

- *Call the phone number in your ad or mailing before you print direct mail materials.* Is it answered properly? Does it work well with the ad claims? Can it answer questions or forward them properly? Is it the right number?!!

- *Feed the kitty.* Federal Post Office regulations require that business reply card or business reply envelope postage be prepaid into a postage account to pay for the reply mail's postage. Many a person has fretted over receiving zero replies, only to find that the Post Office is holding up a ton of mail because nobody has opened or replenished a postage account. The Post Office doesn't allow you to work on credit.

  Failure to receive and log in mail daily causes other problems. If the mail is not processed daily on pickups, the proper response curves of daily replies, or even weekly replies, will be meaningless. This makes it very difficult to forecast.

- *Prepare for proper coding.* In the case of space ads, that means a set-in-type range of testing codes the printer can slug in as a "department" number. For direct mail, that means proper precoding of segments. You can use printed codes on reply cards as long as you know the mailing quantity of each segment. With printed codes you don't have to be concerned about computer printed codes on labels, so you can forego the cost of a window envelope and attach the label directly to the outside.

  At the same time, make sure you have "counts" as to the size of the universe for each test segment *and* the specific segment number of addresses you have received from each universe. These are essential for proper tracking of results.

- *Get it in writing.* Communication between client and agency/vendor is essential where direct mail is used. Everybody is protected and misunderstandings cleared up beforehand, when something can be done without costing an arm and a leg. P.Y.O.R. means protect your own rear. The complexity of direct mail lends itself to more possible errors than most other forms of advertising.

- *Weigh your mailing.*   If you haven't noticed, postage is very expensive. If you are mailing First Class (heaven forbid), it doesn't take much material to go over that one ounce point. The second ounce is almost as expensive. When you weigh, don't forget to include the envelope.

    Naturally, you've got to do this mailing weighing *before* printing. That means a careful weighing is essential. After printing you are stuck.

- *Reply to your mailing.*   This sounds stupid, but I can think of no better way to get the reader's viewpoint. That means copywriters should reply to their copy before the art director sees the project. Copywriters should pretend to be the fulfillment operation, sales force, or whatever job classification receives the response. Ask yourself: "Do I know what to do and can I do it properly?" Do the same thing at the finished layout stage, so that the influence of the graphics can be felt.

Is the reply device efficient? Does it answer the questions we've asked? Most of all, can you *properly* fulfill the request with the information provided?

In summary, maybe you'd better ask yourself one more question. Will the mailing meet its overall objectives? If it doesn't, you won't be meeting yours!

WHY YOU CANNOT GUESS RESPONSE RATES

What response rate will I get?

If someone gives you a definitive answer to the industry's most frequently asked question, don't do business with them.

Why? Because your situation is affected by forces different from those affecting anyone else's, so there is no way the answer can be transferred. Assuming the same product or service, these forces include different media or lists, different economic climate, different season, different merchandise or service, different offers, and a host of other differences. Lastly, your firm is different from their firm in name, image, and so on.

We have clients who can be very successful on a quarter of one percent response. Others have difficulty at seven percent.

But there is something you can do, especially in business mail, to get closer to finding your answer.

A Shortcut to Remember

Let's talk business mail for lead generation, although these principles will apply to many consumer mail situations.

Usually there is an offer. It may be (1) more information, (2) free trial, (3) a free gift, (4) helpful hints, or a host of others.

The sophisticated marketer will realize the best way to get leads is to get the individual, in the sea of up to seven million firms out there, to respond to the bribe and to raise his or her hand and say, "I may be interested in what you have to sell." Thus, the emphasis of the ad or mail piece will be on the offer or bribe—not on what you want to sell.

Now we get to the heart of the problem, which even sophisticated marketers tend to forget when thinking of response rates.

Response will be primarily affected by the offer and not by what you are selling.

It is common sense that a test of two lead generating mailings, for the same product or service, each with a different offer (one is to have a salesperson call and one is an offer of $50 just to try) will generate rather dramatically different response rates.

Remember, your response rates are a function of what you are *offering*, not what you are *selling*.

The Lowest Response Rate May Be the Best

Let's continue with a hypothetical test of two offers: "a salesperson will call" and "$50 just for trying." Obviously, you will get many more $50 replies. Wouldn't you like to pocket a quick $50?

But the business we are in is to make sales. We are not scored by the number of leads we generate. Two leads generating one sale is better than a hundred leads generating one sale!

Some will say that almost any lead is a good lead because the prospect may buy later and we've been able to tell our story. At $300 per sales call, that is pretty expensive. I'm pretty conservative in my old age and tend to count only "cash-on-the-barrelhead" sales, classifying future sales as pleasant surprises.

Keeping Track of Conversions

The trick is how to keep track of conversions to sales versus no conversions. There are many ways in which to handle this, but a good rule of thumb to remember is: No person will ever give credit to a lead as a source of a sale. It's always that person's salesmanship, ingenuity, and so on.

How good is your lead program? Shut off the leads for a while. See if the field raises a ruckus! If not, maybe your leads really are lousy and you'd better get your act together.

FIFTEEN

ORDER FORMS

WHY ORDER FORMS ARE SO IMPORTANT

Everyone wants his or her product on sale by the checkout register at a supermarket. Obviously, it is the ultimate point-of-sale impulse buy position. The golden square foot! Merchandisers know its worth and will almost kill for it.

Mail order professionals haven't scratched the surface of the potential of their impulse buy position—the order form.

Average Order Size Key to Success

Mail order professionals realize their best chance for increased profits is to increase their average order. That means either selling up or selling more. And selling more can either mean more of the same or of different items.

In today's world of high fixed and variable costs, unless you are increasing the average order in your business, you will soon go out of business. Most of the mail order failures I've traced have failed primarily because they couldn't or didn't bother to try to get their average order up.

Seven Ways Your Order Form Can Increase Your Average Order

By the time readers of your mail order catalog or mailing package get involved with your order form, they have decided to buy. What better time to sell them *more*? Here are a few successful ways you may find. (Remember, your order form can be expanded to foldout pages at a very low cost.)

1. *Last minute news/hot item flash.*   Readers always have greater interest in what is the latest. An order form is a natural place to reinforce a "last minute" item. Because it is printed in black only, the reader suspects it is probably printed at the last minute. Thus the promotional point for latest news makes sense.

2. *President's or merchandiser's favorites.*   Most letters from presidents or owners of catalogs are very dry and don't take the opportunity for a strong call to action. If the respected merchandiser singles out a few items he feels are important, they will sell. It doesn't matter that they just happened to be items clogging up the warehouse!

3. *Liners.*   By adding 20 to 100 items to your catalog order form, just line listed like a laundry list, you will generate impulse sales. The secret is to use only those items that are fully explained by their names or by three or four additional words, with no illustrations. Examples are "Four Titlist Golf Balls," "Apple Corers," "Vice Grip Pliers," and so on.

4. *Volume discounts.*   If you have done your math correctly, you can afford to spend more to increase your average order be-

cause you have already covered most of your overhead and expenses. Incremental costing makes sense. "Ten percent off on all purchases over $100" can make sense to the reader. It is also a justification for him to spend more money with you.

5.   *Gift packaging.*   Very special packaging does work at specialty retail stores. It can work just as well with mail. Catalogers forget to show a really gorgeous four-color picture of the special package. That special package, priced right, can generate more gross profit than an item of merchandise. Test it.

6.   *Sale–sale–sale.*   The order form, with expanding pages, is ideal for sale merchandise. The lesser quality of most order form paper makes the placement of items on sale a natural.

7.   *Simple and smooth-flowing order form.*   If your order form is simple and easy to fill out, you not only increase your chances of larger orders but also decrease the chance for errors.

WHY YOU SHOULD LOOK AT YOUR ORDER FORM LIKE A BAR OF SOAP

You will increase your responses if you market your order card or coupon like you'd market a bar of soap.

George Wiedemann, who was circulation director of *Time* for many years, and now heads up Grey Advertising's direct marketing operation, expounded this concept during a fascinating dinner discussion on what direct marketing is all about.

George is right. Today, one couponed ad or one mailing piece is not enough to get the most out of marketing a product or service to consumers. If your list or audience potential is over one million, "multimedia" is all important. Too many of us throw this term around without grasping the meaning and potential impact of a sound "multimedia" program.

To understand, let us say we are offering a magazine subscription. It used to be that a well thought-out mailing once or twice a year was enough. Now there are literally hundreds of magazines being offered. The competition has become fierce. Previous mail order buyers and subscribers to other publications are the market to which these mailings are targeted. Because they respond better, they are also targets for mailers of many other products or services. There is a lot of competition in the mailboxes of the better prospects. No matter how attractive, one mail package cannot do it as well as with outside support impact.

Other media are used to create a positive feeling about a particular mailing piece, so that when you do scan your mail on its way to the wastebasket you will stop and open it. Television and radio do the best job of this, just like they do for a bar of soap.

George likens a mailbox to a grocery store shelf. There are a lot of different soaps there, just as there are a lot of different items in your mailbox. Or, extending the concept further, "multimedia" efforts may enhance the competitiveness of direct response ads within the magazine or newspaper you are reading. Just as television reminds you of a particular bar of soap at your point of decision in the grocery store, direct marketing can remind you at your point of decision at the mailbox or in the middle of your favorite magazine.

This marketing support is not limited to television and radio—everything from newspaper inserts to subscription cards also works.

Repetition is another form of support. Seeing the same offer more frequently, or in different formats, furthers the positive image of that item in your mind. It is like what the catalog people say—"I'm going to repeat all my popular items. Because if that many people bought, just think how many people *almost* bought."

This multimedia concept is not for everyone. You have to work out your numbers. Television or radio support is expensive when you are targeting to a small audience. Obviously, a high penetration of the market by your mailing is in order.

The more I think of Wiedemann's bar of soap analogy towards "multimedia," the more I realize the similarity to direct mail principles is beyond just multimedia support. A package on the shelf versus another brand is an impulse decision, made rapidly and subconsciously. It is really no different than the impulse decision to pause, read a direct marketing ad, and respond. Perhaps we are really in the same business but with different points of sale.

Too many people in the direct marketing industry have said that commercial retail marketers don't know anything about direct response. Maybe they know more than we do. Anybody out there from P&G or Lever who wants to give us a hand?

SIXTEEN

ADVERTISING AGENCIES

WHY THE 15% AGENCY COMMISSION DOES NOT WORK

Advertising agencies have traditionally charged their clients 15%. What this means in television, radio, newspapers, and magazines is that you, as the advertiser, pay the agency the stated rates, but the agency sends the specific paper, magazine, or station the stated sum less 15%.

In addition, it is general agency practice to charge their clients a 17.65% markup on all production. That means buy-outs or out-of-pocket expenses such as typesetting, photography, illustrations, recording, filming, and so on.

It wouldn't be too far out of line to say that when budgeting general or traditional advertising, 10% or 20% of the media budget is reserved for these production items. Because the same ads are run in media over and over again, with little or no extra agency effort, this compensation was adequate.

Direct marketing advertising agencies cannot work on this basis and stay in business. Let us list some of the reasons, as they relate to direct mail.

1. *Postage is not commissionable.* The post office is a medium, yet it does not pay commissions. In consumer mailings, postage may be 25% to 40% of the total package cost. Therefore, agencies must charge more to make up for this loss.

2. *Conventional advertising is finding the traditional 15% inadequate.* Many have gone to a fee basis or a combination of fees and commissions. Understanding why the 15% is adequate in general agency work helps to understand why direct marketing cannot live with 15%. Some of general advertising's reasons include:

A. The increasing specialization and segmentation offered by media. This includes utilizing the more efficient regional or demographic sections of magazines and newspapers, rather than the entire run. It includes the use of smaller, more targeted media, such as small circulation consumer and trade publications. There are more radio, cable TV, and other stations than ever before to divide up the market.

B. The increasing complexity of creative to match media segmentation. The more tailored creative can be to match segmented media, the more effective.

C. The increasing trend to tie advertising to dealers. Dealers share in these programs. Coordinated dealer advertising increases its efficiency. These dealer programs require far greater production and supervisory time.

3. *Direct mail is far more complex.* More complex than a newspaper or magazine advertisement. First, in magazines and

newspapers all you have to prepare is the material to be put on the page. The publication has the responsibility for printing, audience, and delivery.

Second, direct mail is far more complex. You often have an envelope, a reply envelope, a letter, a brochure, a reply card, and sometimes a premium. All these pieces have to fit together physically and in a harmonious way. They all have to be completed at the same time. So there are many more chances for error. And what can go wrong, usually does go wrong . . . and at the most inopportune time. There are also the problems of list ordering.

It is my belief that it takes a greater skill creatively and administratively to cope with these problems.

4. *Direct mail goes to small audiences.* Because it is a personal medium, the greater the list is segmented and pared down, the greater the response, the smaller the mailing. Similarly, the more sophisticated the mailing, the more versions.

5. *Direct mail's propensity to test.* It is not unusual to be simultaneously testing several lists, two or three different mailing packages and different offers. All this takes more creative time and more administrative time to do it correctly.

6. *The greater complexity of list selection.* There are over 40,000 mailing lists on the market. That far exceeds the total of newspapers, magazines, radio, and television stations. Good media selection is far less difficult than list selection.

Then, often in list selection you must also do list merging and purging to remove duplicates. This takes extra expertise and time.

7. *The greater cost of an error.* Direct mail costs 10 to 100 times as much as print media. The list of a piece printed incorrectly is far more costly. There are also many more places for error in direct mail.

8. *The "one shot" nature of direct mail.* More often than not,

direct mail pieces are a one time shot. There are rarely continued mailings of the same content. If there are, there is often little the agency can be compensated. In general advertising, the agency gets full compensation each time the ad is run, change or no change.

One of the main reasons that mailing packages do not repeat themselves is the fact that testing is usually included in every mailing. These test results invariably lead to package change and improvement. This takes creative and administrative time.

9. *Purchasing complexity.*   Media has one rate for what you want to do. In direct mail, many printers can provide the same product and no two printers will quote the same price. That means many more phone calls.

In addition, there are almost unlimited paper combinations. Each of these paper stocks are priced differently. And, to make it worse, they change their prices frequently and are often un-available. So you have to start all over with a different paper or a different source.

10. *Distribution.*   General media handles everything. But, in direct mail, the mailer must put on the labels, zip sequence the mailing, insert the pieces, seal the package, add the postage, and deliver the mail to the post office.

11. *Time and risk.*   All the aforementioned comes down to time and risk.

Time is involved in every step. It takes time and skill to do all of these tasks. The skill required is at the agency level. The work is not farmed out—it must be done in-house.

There is far greater risk in direct mail. There are many more places for mistakes because the agency is responsible for more aspects than in general advertising, where the printing, paper, and distribution are the responsibility of the media.

There Is No Such Thing as a Free Lunch!

Direct mail takes greater skill, which is perhaps why there is such a shortage of good people in the business. The skill of a *good,* seasoned practitioner becomes more important than in any other medium because of its expense and complexity. It saves money to use a good, experienced professional.

SEVENTEEN

COSTS AND SCHEDULES

WHY DIRECT MAIL COST ESTIMATING IS DIFFICULT

You place space in a magazine and you know your exact cost. You place a direct mail effort and estimates are all over the map. You don't know what to do. You lose confidence in direct mail. You shouldn't. Direct mail is infinitely more complex than other print media.

When you place space in a magazine, it is really very simple. The magazine doesn't really care what is on your page. They only care about size, color, and region, if there are regional splits offered. The shape of the magazine isn't going to change. The size selections you have are few. All the magazine has to do is fit the geometric pieces together.

Further, the paper is the same throughout the magazine. It is

215

printed all at once. It is going to be delivered to the same audience (subscribers) and the same number of newsstands.

Now, let's look at direct mail. First, you have the problem of format. There are endless combinations of shapes and sizes your mailing could be utilizing. So here comes the first problem. The format cannot be decided until the creative direction and graphics support are determined. If you predetermine the creative effort, in terms of format, before the graphics have been worked out, you are unnecessarily limiting the freedom of the creative people to do their best job.

Next you have the problem of the exact number of pieces mailed. If you are testing, you have no problem because you can predetermine the number of pieces mailed. But if you are mailing out entire house (customer) lists, or want to reach all of a certain category of business, or reach all homes within a radius of a certain location, you probably do not know just how many names will be available. How can you figure printing costs if you don't know how many pieces you are going to print?

Next you have the problem of changes. As the number of pieces within a mail package go up arithmetically, the number of changes often go up geometrically. In other words, there can be a domino effect in direct mail. If you change the theme of the letter, for example, you will have to redo the envelope copy and the response card copy. Changes are inevitable, because as you tighten up copy, graphics, or the product, or if service has a change due to the dynamics of the marketplace, they often require complete rethinking, rather than patching.

There is another factor. Direct mail usually tells much more of a story. That has two ramifications. There are usually many more pictures and much more type than in other forms of print advertising. In addition, because of the greater detail, there is much more exposure to change.

Finally, there is the nature of printing. You may get lucky and find a printer who has an idle press and will take your job below cost. You may be unlucky and find that all presses are busy and quotes are based upon the overtime that the printer knows must be paid to squeeze you in.

Steps to Better Understanding

1. *Set the broadest parameters possible.*   Usually a range of costs or a preliminary ball park estimate makes sense. This accomplishes two things. It protects the budget and gives the creative people a feel for their limitations as far as quality, complexity, and size are concerned.

2. *Allow yourself a contingency.*   Plus or minus 10% is not a bad figure to use. Be careful what you use as your contingency base. This percentage should be applied *after* taking into consideration the normal amount of changes, and build that into your base figure, not the contingency.

3. *Allow maximum time for the job.*   Last minute crash programs can cost you dearly. Not only will vendors' prices go up, but there will be a greater tendency for mistakes on everyone's part. The faster you go may really come out to mean the slower you go.

This leads to my pet peeve: "We don't have time to fix it because it is late." I've found, in most cases, doing the major parts right is more important than getting it out on time ineffectively.

4. *Concentrate on the important aspects.*   Costs can be reduced and estimates lived up to if changes are kept to a minimum. Perhaps 50% of all the changes I've ever seen were unnecessary. They may have been sound in the maker's mind, but they were usually either of a nature where the change was a very minor point or where there was no correct way—it was the result of a subjective feeling.

5.   *Use professionals.*   The fees or commissions that a professional person, organization, or agency charges are usually more than saved because they know (1) the short cuts, (2) the pitfalls, (3) which printer may be hungry, (4) that an expensive direct mail piece doesn't necessarily mean an effective direct mail piece, and (5) how to negotiate with vendors in crisis situations.

Many advertisers feel they are not doing their job if they don't do it all themselves. Competent direct marketing advertisers know that proper delegation and putting their time and efforts into data gathering pays off.

6.   *Get all the facts at the start.*   This is, perhaps, the most costly aspect of direct marketing. People tend to be lazy, too busy, or afraid to ask their superiors or other parts of the organization for too much information. They feel they are expected to know everything. Watch out for a person who is supposed to know everything! Unless the people who execute direct mail have all the facts, they can't do the best job. The needed facts will appear sooner or later. It may be when the president looks at the final art, all neatly pasted together with all photography executed. At this point, changes are really costly.

7.   *Look over past jobs.*   The mailing you are now doing may have been executed before you became involved with the company or department. If you take the time to look up and assemble the costs, you may find that the job was similar to one which had already been produced. Just add the costs for inflation and you'll probably come out with a pretty good estimate.

8.   *Tell your vendors and others involved more than you think they need to know.*   If they understand the total picture, they have less chance for error and more chance for better advertising.

Good estimating is up to you!

EIGHTEEN

CONCLUSION

WHY YOU WILL BE SUCCESSFUL WITH DIRECT MARKETING

Above all, because you have read this book!

No, not because of what this book says. But if you've read through to this point, you've shown three very important characteristics that will keep you a step ahead: the desire to *learn*, the *interest*, and the *"why."*

Most books are read by a small segment of the population. What we see coming out of high schools and colleges indicates the problem will be getting worse. People are too lazy (usually expressed as too busy) to read. Reading is knowledge and knowledge is growth—growth to do what you want to do better than ever.

If you've read this book, the chances are you've read other books, which combined are giving you knowledge, perhaps a broad knowledge. You've got the instinct and drive to learn.

Direct marketing is especially compatible with those who thrive on the learning experience. It's true because direct marketing gives you the answers. It provides a greater learning experience than other forms of advertising and marketing because it gives so many answers.

Your dedication to reading, and thus learning, will provide added insights for your supervisory or editorial responsibilities in the fields of copyediting, direction, and execution. Reading helps in so many ways.

Direct marketing, especially direct mail, generates an enormous amount of paper work—more than other forms of advertising. If there is more paper work, there is more reading and more opportunity to learn. Because you are the type that takes the time to read and learn, you have a talent very important to direct marketing success. Interest.

Direct marketing, direct mail, and telephone are truly not the glamour media of the industry. Television, radio, and magazines are certainly more glamorous.

Reading this book and others on direct marketing shows you care to be more knowledgeable about this business. You must enjoy what you do. There are a lot of people out there who don't give direct marketing its share of the spotlight.

There are many who think of "junk mail" and "junk telephone," rather than thinking about the opportunities for greater personalization and targeting that these media provide.

Our industry has shown that those practitioners who are dedicated to direct marketing take the time to understand it.

Understanding "why" is important. It is not enough to just know the rules, or repeat what has been done before. It is vital to consistently try to do better. When the present status, no matter how satisfactory it may be, is always questioned as to how it can be better, you have the basis of the direct marketing business.

"Let's test it." What other forms of marketing do as much testing as direct marketing? Everything is tested. Lists, price, copy, graphics, offer, timing, publications, frequency, recency, monetary, audience segments, format, theme, and much, much more.

No other form of marketing does as much testing and provides so much data that can find the better answers to the "whys" that are raised with almost every answer.

We are all very fortunate to be a part of this exciting medium because we have the opportunity to share in the *understanding of direct marketing.*

It leaves us with two lifetime responsibilities—to continue to test and find more answers and to share those answers with our industry.

You, too, can leave your mark.

INDEX